LEGAL ISSUES JOURNAL

Volume 3 Issue 2 July 2015

www.uklsa.co.uk/law-review

Legal Issues is an international journal managed and published by the UK Law Students' Association (UKLSA). The Journal publishes fine research in all fields of law on the basis of its contribution to the society, originality, interdisciplinary interest, and elegance. *Legal Issues* also provides important news and interpretation on changes in the legal world and coming trends affecting law, lawyers, and society. The Journal's primary aims are two. First, to facilitate a forum for the sharing of knowledge, news, and trends concerning the application of the law throughout the globe and for further development in all fields of law. Second, to ensure the dissemination of fine accessible work to the public throughout the world.

ISBN-13: 978-1514857861
ISBN-10: 1514857863
ISSN 2050-005X (Online)

The United Kingdom Law Students' Association

http://www.uklsa.co.uk

Divisions

Academic Division
Publications Division
Equalities Division
Careers Division
Schools Division

Contents

ARTICLES

CASE COMMENT

IN SEARCH OF 'JOINT CRIMINAL ENTERPRISE' IN THE INTERNATIONAL CRIMES (TRIBUNALS) ACT 1973

Muhsina Farhat Chowdhury[1]

There is a need for a resonance of the doctrine of joint criminal enterprise (hereinafter, JCE) in the International Crimes (Tribunals) Act, 1973. Thus, this paper explores whether or not the 1973 Act accommodates the provision of joint criminal enterprise. There is substantial presence of the basic and systematic forms of JCE in the criminal jurisprudence of Bangladesh. Reasons are three-fold. First, the doctrine of JCE was already a settled principle of criminal liability in the criminal jurisprudence of Bangladesh during 1971; second, this doctrine in the form of common purpose liability was in practice in the post-World War II international tribunals and national courts trying international crimes of similar nature; third, the ICT Act by its very nature, purpose and language, accommodates the principle of JCE.

Keywords: Joint criminal enterprise, International Crimes Tribunal, Bangladesh

1. INTRODUCTION

From being the 'magic weapon'[2] of prosecutors to try the accused of international crimes, to the 'darling of critics', 'joint criminal enterprise'

---

[1] LLM, International Law, University of Cambridge; member of the International Crimes Strategy Forum (ICSF); former researcher for the Office of the Prosecution at the International Crimes Tribunals of Bangladesh.

[2] Kai Ambos described this doctrine as magic weapon. *See* Kai Ambos, "Joint Criminal Enterprise and Command Responsibility", Journal of International Criminal Justice, Vol. 5, No. 1, 2007, pp. 159-183, 159.

(hereinafter, JCE) has emerged as one of the most discussed doctrines of international criminal law. The doctrine of JCE has been derived out of individual criminal responsibility,[3] which imposes the criminal liability upon an individual within a joint enterprise that commits crime with a common criminal purpose or common criminal objective. In this regard Kai Ambos observed that, 'the JCE doctrine serves to impute certain criminal acts or results to persons for their participation in a collective (joint) criminal enterprise'.[4] Thus, joint criminal enterprise is a group of persons that acts towards a common objective with a common plan. This common plan may develop through 'explicit or tacit' agreement between the persons.[5] Thus, in this doctrine all those, who knowingly participate in and contribute to the realization of common criminal purpose, where a pre-existing plan to commit core international crimes exists, or where there is evidence that the members of a group are acting with a common criminal purpose, may be held individually criminally responsible.[6] In addition, this doctrine also makes criminally liable such perpetrators of crimes which were intended or committed, but were also a natural and foreseeable consequence of the common purpose or the purpose of the joint enterprise.[7] Therefore, 'the combined, associated or common criminal purpose of the participants in the enterprise' is the fundamental principle of JCE.[8]

The doctrine of JCE was raised to prominence though the ICTY[9] Appeal Chamber decision in *Prosecutor vs. Tadić*.[10] The necessity of this liability doctrine arose due to the very nature of international crimes committed during wartime. Admittedly, international crimes, i.e. war crimes, crimes against

---

[3] Allison Martson Danner and Jenny S. Martinez, "Guilty Associations: Joint Criminal Enterprise, Command Responsibility, and the Development of International Criminal Law", *California Law Review,* Vol. 93, Issue. 2, 2005, pp. 75-169, 102.

[4] Kai Ambos, "Amicus Curiae Brief in the Matter of the Co-Prosecutors' Appeal of the Closing Order Against KAING Guek Eav "DUCH" dated 8 August 2008", *Criminal Law Forum,* Vol. 20, No. 2-3, 2009, pp. 353-388, 353.

[5] *Id.*

[6] Ciara Damgaard, "The Joint Criminal Enterprise Doctrine: A Monster Theory of Liability or a Legitimate and Satisfactory Tool in the Prosecution of the Perpetrators of Core International Crimes?", in *Individual Criminal Responsibility for Core International Crimes,* Springer, Heidelberg, 2008, pp. 127-358, 127.

[7] *Id.*

[8] Kia Ambos, 2009, 353, *op. cit.*

[9] International Criminal Tribunal for the Former Yugoslavia.

[10] *Prosecutor vs. Dusko Tadić,* Appeals Chamber, International Criminal Tribunal for the Former Yogoslavia, IT-94-1-I, Judgment, July 15, 1999. André Klip and Göran Sluiter, eds., *Annotated Leading Cases of International Criminal Tribunals, Volume VIII: The International Criminal Tribunal for the Former Yugoslavia 2001-2002*, Hart Publishing, Oxford, 2005, 368.

humanity, crimes against peace, genocide are 'mass crimes'[11] committed against 'large masses of people, often stretched across large geographical areas'[12] and they are committed in a 'collective, widespread and systematic context'[13]. In this regard the *Tadić* Appeal Chamber has rightfully observed that:

> [m]ost of the time these crimes do not result from the criminal propensity of single individuals but constitute manifestations of collective criminality: the crimes are often carried out by groups of individuals acting in pursuance of a common criminal design[14].

Therefore, if only the physical perpetrators of crime are held liable as principle offender, then the critical role of other co-perpetrators, who were part of the common criminal plan, as well as the moral gravity of their behavior, would be disregarded.[15] Thus this doctrine of criminal liability[16] enables bringing to justice those perpetrators of international crimes, who acted at various levels of a common criminal plan and in different capacities, to achieve a final and common criminal design.[17]

Moreover, wartime international crimes are committed in such an intricate context that it is often not easy to identify the personal contributions of individuals in a collective criminal enterprise.[18] All participants do not act in the same manner, and instead play different roles in planning, organizing, instigating, coordinating, executing or otherwise contributing to the criminal conduct.[19] Furthermore the evidence relating to each individual's conduct may

---

[11] Allen O'Rourke, "Recent Development. Joint Criminal Enterprise and Brdanin: Misguided Over-correction", Harvard International Law Journal, Vol. 47, No. 1, Winter 2006, pp. 307-325, 307.

[12] *Id.*

[13] Kia Ambos, 2009, 355, *op. cit.*

[14] *Prosecutor vs. Dusko Tadic,* July 15, 1999, para. 191, *op. cit.*

[15] Giulia Bigi, "Joint Criminal Enterprise in the Jurisprudence of the International Criminal Tribunal for the Former Yugoslavia and the Prosecution of Senior Political and Military Leaders: The *Krajišnik* case", Max Planck Yearbook of United Nations Laws, Vol. 14, 2010, pp. 51-83, 53.

[16] *JCE is not a crime but a form of criminal liability. See,* Amicus Curiae Brief on Professor Antonio Cassese and Members of the Journal of International Criminal Justice on Joint Criminal Enterprise Doctrine, in *Co-Prosecutors vs. KAING Guek Eav alias "DUCH",* Pre-trial Chamber, Extraordinary Chambers in the Courts of Cambodia, 001/18-07-2007-ECCC/OCIJ, October 27, 2008, para. 20.

[17] Giulia Bigi, 2010, 53, *op. cit.*

[18] *Co-Prosecutors vs. KAING Guek Eav alias "DUCH",* October 27, 2008, para. 20, *op. cit.*

[19] Antonio Cassese, "The Proper Limits of Individual Criminal Responsibility under the Doctrine of Joint Criminal Enterprise", Journal of International Criminal Justice, Vol. 5, No. 1, 2007, pp. 109-133, 110.

prove difficult if not impossible to find.[20] Thus it would be a grave infringement of justice if the perpetrators of collective crimes go unpunished due to the non-availability of evidence surrounding individual participation. It is in this regard that the doctrine of JCE is crucial, because it is one of the most effective tools for convicting individuals of core international crimes where there is no direct evidence of the actual perpetration of the accused regarding the crime in question.[21] Gustafson correctly notes:

> [j]oint criminal enterprise doctrine can enhance the truth-telling functions of international criminal law trials by portraying, more accurately than other theories of liability, how crimes are conceived of, planned and executed in a system-criminality context.[22]

However, a question may arise that since there are other modes of criminal liability in international criminal law, i.e. aiding-abetting, which imposes liability on other indirect actors of crimes, then the need for JCE? This query calls for a brief comparison between JCE and aiding-abetting. Aiding and abetting is different from JCE, in the sense that the former 'requires contribution with substantial effect on the participation of the crime, whereas the latter simply requires acts to the furtherance of the common plan'.[23] Further, the *mens rea* of the former demands knowledge that the acts performed assisted in the commission of the crime, while the latter demands intent to pursue the common purpose or such intent plus foresight that crimes outside the common purpose are likely to be committed.[24] Thus, it is evident that with the requirement of substantial contribution to the commission of crimes, aiding and abetting results in a lesser degree of culpability compared to commission through JCE.[25] A distinction between conspiracy and JCE is also essential in order to clear the confusion between these two doctrines. Although there are similarities between these two doctrines, JCE is distinct and very different.[26] In this respect, David Hunt affirmed:

---

[20] *Id.*

[21] Ciara Damgaard, 2008, 127, *op. cit.*

[22] Katrina Gustafson, "The Requirement of an 'Expressed Agreement' for Joint Criminal Enterprise Liability, A Critique of Brdanin", Journal of International Criminal Justice, Vol. 5, No. 1, 2007, pp. 134-158, 139.

[23] *Co-Prosecutors vs. KAING Guek Eav alias "DUCH"*, October 27, 2008, para. 28, *op. cit.*

[24] *Id.*

[25] *Id.*

[26] Michael A. Glazer, "Where an Ongoing Joint Criminal Enterprise exists, What is necessary to bring about its termination as a matter of law or to terminate an individual's membership in the Joint Criminal Enterprise?", *Case Western Reserve School of Law, International War Crimes Research Lab,* Spring 2006, 25, available at: http://law.case.edu/war-crimes-research-portal/ memoranda/ glazer_ michael.pdf

> Conspiracy is not a mode of individual criminal responsibility for the commission of a crime. Conspiracy is itself a crime, which is complete once the agreement between the conspirators has been reached. … On the other hand, joint criminal enterprise is available as one mode of individual criminal responsibility by which a crime may be committed, but only where the agreed (or contemplated) crime has been in fact committed.[27]

Now, keeping in mind the abovementioned qualities of *JCE,* this paper would like to search for a resonance of the doctrine of JCE in the *International Crimes (Tribunals) Act*, 1973. The *ICT Act* was adopted by the Parliament of Bangladesh to provide for the detention, prosecution and punishment of persons for genocide, crimes against humanity, war crimes and other crimes under international law.[28] Although, this Act deals with international crimes, the tribunal(s) it constitutes is not international. It is purely a national legislation to try crimes of international nature committed within the territory of Bangladesh and thus the tribunal(s) constituted under it is also domestic.[29] However, an interesting trait of this Act can be traced from the parliamentary debates on *International Crimes (Tribunals) Bill* in 1973, where it is stated that all the principles of international law and known norms of justice, existing till 1973, have been incorporated into it.[30] Here, it is important to note that this incorporation of principles of international law, does not affect the domestic nature of the tribunal, rather after passing of the Bill, those principles became part of the Bangladeshi national law.

Thus, this paper argues that the doctrine of JCE does indeed have scope in the *ICT Act.* The reason behind this is three-fold: first of all, the doctrine of JCE was already a settled principle of criminal liability in the criminal jurisprudence of Bangladesh during 1971; secondly, this doctrine in the form of common purpose liability was in practice in the post-World War II international tribunals and national courts trying international crimes of similar nature; third, the *ICT Act* by its very nature, purpose and language, accommodates the principle of JCE. By determining the extent of the three

---

[27] Jens Meierhenrich, "Conspiracy in International Law", *Annual Review of Law and Social Science,* Vol. 2, December 2006, pp. 341-357, pp. 350-351.

[28] Preamble to the *International Crimes (Tribunals) Act,* 1973.

[29] International Crimes Strategy Forum (ICSF), "Stephen Rapp: Of misconceptions, unrealistic expectations and double standards", May 22, 2011, in Opinion page of bdnews24.com, available at: http://opinion.bdnews24.com/2011/05/22/stephen-rapp-of-misconceptions-unrealistic-expectations-and-double-standards/

[30] Mr. Serajul Huq in Parliamentary Debates on International Crimes (Tribunals) Bill, 1973, Vol. 2, No. 37, 2356.

forms of JCE, i.e. basic, systematic and extended,[31] this paper will determine which form of JCE the *ICT Act* accommodates.

2. A Brief Synopsis of the Doctrine of Joint Criminal Enterprise

In order to get a brief idea on the origins of JCE, the paper relies on the ICTY and post ICTY case laws. Although the principle of JCE originated in the post-World War II legislations and case laws under the heads of other names[32], it primarily came under scrutiny through the case of *Dusko Tadić* in the ICTY. As noted by the Trial Chamber in *Prosecutor vs. Radoslav Brdanin & Momir Talic,* the Appeals Chamber's decision in *Prosecutor vs. Dusko Tadić*[33] is the first contemporary recognition of the doctrine.[34] Here it is worthy of noting that the phrases 'joint criminal enterprise' or 'common criminal purpose' or 'common criminal plan' are not explicitly mentioned in the *Statute of the International Criminal Tribunal for the Former Yugoslavia.* The Appeals Chamber defined 'committed'[35] to encompass not only those who physically participated in the commission of the crimes but also those who contributed to the crime's commission in execution of a common criminal purpose or joint criminal enterprise.[36] It came to this observation on the basis of 'teleological interpretation'[37] of Article 7(1)[38], which considered the intention to cover all those responsible for international crimes in the Former Yugoslavia.[39] However, this interpretation of *Tadić* Appeals Chamber

---

[31] Marja Lehto, *Indirect Responsibility for Terrorist Acts: Redefinition of the Concept of Terrorism Beyond Violent Acts*, Martinus Nijhoff Publishers, Boston, 2010, 132.

[32] Common criminal purpose, common criminal plan, common design or purpose, common criminal design, common purpose, common design or common concerted design.

[33] *Prosecutor vs. Dusko Tadic*, July 15, 1999, para. 191, *op. cit.*

[34] *Prosecutor vs. Radoslav Brdanin & Momir Talic,* Decision on Form of Further Amended Indictment and Prosecution Application to Amend, Trial Chamber II, International Criminal Tribunal for the Former Yugoslavia, IT-99-36/1, June 26, 2001, para. 36.

[35] This word was taken from Article 7 (1) of the ICTY Statute.

[36] Mohamed Elewa Badar, "Participation in Crimes in the Jurisprudence of the ICTY and ICTR", in *Routledge Handbook of International Criminal Law,* edited by William A. Schabas and Nadia Bernaz, Routledge, Oxon, 2011, pp. 245-267, 252.

[37] It is a method of interpretation, which looks at the values and purpose of the legislation that are implicit in the text.

[38] A person who planned, instigated, ordered, committed or otherwise aided and abetted in the planning, preparation or execution of a crime referred to in articles 2 to 5 of the present Statute, shall be individually responsible for the crime.

[39] André Klip and Göran Sluiter, eds., 2005, 368, *op. cit.*

was subsequently affirmed in other trials of the ICTY as well as the ICTR[40] and, the SCSL[41].

Antonio Cassese identified that the doctrine of JCE can take three different forms[42]: basic (JCE I), systematic (JCE II) and extended (JCE III). First, the basic mode of liability arises when all participants shared the common intent to the concerned crime although only some of them may have physically perpetrated the crime.[43] It is a responsibility for acts agreed upon when making the common criminal plan or purpose.[44] Second, the systematic mode of liability is concerned with crimes committed by members of military or administrative units on the basis of common criminal plan or purpose, for instance crimes implemented in concentration camps or detention centers.[45] And third, the extended mode of liability arises where some extra crimes have been committed beyond the common plan or purpose, but the extra criminal act was nonetheless a natural and foreseeable consequence to the perpetrator of the common plan.[46] In the above three forms of JCE the standard of *actus reus* or subjective element is similar: a) plurality of persons; b) the existence of a common plan, design or purpose, which amounts to or involves the commission of a crime provided for in the statute; and c) participation of the accused in the common design.[47]

This 'plurality of persons' does not need to be an organized group of individuals. Thus, the plurality of persons element is satisfied when the prosecution proves that the group 'included the leaders of political bodies, the army, and the police who held power (in a given area)' without showing that persons in these disparate groups were acting together in an organized fashion.[48] Moreover, for the existence of a common plan or purpose, there is no necessity for the plan to have been arranged or formulated previously. It satisfies the requirements of subjective elements, if the plan is formulated extemporaneously.[49] However, the condition of common criminal purpose is not satisfied, if alleged JCE members committed crimes for reasons of personal revenge, rather than to effectuate a criminal purpose shared with others, even

---

[40]International Criminal Tribunal for Rwanda.
[41] The Special Court of Sierra Leone.
[42] Antonio Cassese, 2007, 111, *op. cit.*
[43] *Id.*
[44] *Id.*
[45] Kai Ambos, 2009, 160, *op. cit.*
[46] *Id.*
[47] Catherine H. Gibson, "Testing the Legitimacy of the Joint Criminal Enterprise Doctrine in the ICTY: A Comparison of Individual Liability for Group Conduct in International and Domestic Law", Duke Journal of Comparative and International Law, Vol. 18, No. 2, 2008, pp. 521-547, 524.
[48] *Id,* quoting *Prosecutor v. Milomir Stakic*, Appeals Chamber, International Criminal Tribunal for the Former Yugoslavia, IT-97-24-A, Judgment, March 22, 2006, para. 69.
[49] *Prosecutor vs. Dusko Tadic*, July 15, 1999, para. 227, *op. cit.*

when these crimes are committed systematically.[50] Furthermore, the 'participation' requirement does not indicate physical participation, rather it implies assistance in, or contribution to, the executions of the common plan or purpose.[51] And this participation has to be voluntary. Consequent to this observation, later case laws have increased the level of participation by introducing the 'significant' factor to it. In a case, the Appeal Chamber of the ICTY observed that, 'the act in furtherance must be significant'.[52] And in order to be significant participation the accused must be, 'a cog in the wheel of events leading up to the result which in fact occurred'.[53]

Although, in terms of subjective elements there is no significant difference between these three forms of JCE, they vary from each other through *mens rea* or objective elements. For JCE I, the *mens rea* simply requires that the perpetrator acted with the intent to perpetrate a certain crime[54]. Here, 'intent to perpetrate' implies common shared intent of the members of the enterprise. Whereas, the requisite *mens rea* for JCE II is two fold: a) personal knowledge of the system of ill treatment; and b) the intent to further this common concerned system of ill treatment.[55] Here it is worthy of noting that, since JCE II involves a large number of people in an organized system, the *means rea* must be assessed in relation to the knowledge of a particular accused.[56] Now, being completely distinctive in terms of *mens rea,* JCE III requires following of two steps to achieve its objective element. First, the accused must have the intention to participate in and contribute to the common criminal purpose; and second, the accused must also know that a crime may be perpetrated by a member of the group and willingly join or continue to participate in the enterprise knowing that the crime might occur.[57]

---

[50] Catherine H. Gibson, 2008, 524, *op. cit.;* quoting *Prosecutor v. Fatmir Limaj*, Appeals Chamber, International Criminal Tribunal for the Former Yugoslavia, IT-03-66-A, September 27, 2007, para. 113-115.

[51] *Prosecutor vs. Dusko Tadic,* July 15, 1999, para. 227, *op. cit.*

[52] *Prosecutor vs. Miroslav Kvoka et al.,* Trial Chamber, International Criminal Tribunal for the Former Yugoslavia, IT-98-30/1-T, Judgment, November 2, 2001, para. 309.

[53] *Prosecutor vs. Radoslav Brdanin & Momir Talic,* Appeal Chamber, International Criminal Tribunal for the Former Yugoslavia, IT-99-36-A, April 3, 2007, para. 427; quoting *Trial of Feurstein and others,* Proceedings of a War Crimes Trial held at Hamburg, Germany (August 4-24, 1948), Judgment, August 24, 1948, at. 7.

[54] *Prosecutor vs. Dusko Tadic,* July 15, 1999, para. 228, *op. cit.*

[55] *Id.*

[56] *Prosecutor v. Miroslav Kvocka et al.*, Appeals Chamber, International Criminal Tribunal for the Former Yugoslavia, IT-98-30/A-A, Judgment, February 28, 2005, para. 86.

[57] *Ibid.,* para. 8. Due to this extended nature of JCE III in terms of *mens rea,* it has been a target of critics from the very beginning. However, discussion on this criticism would be reserved for another paper.

3. Seeking the Doctrine in the Criminal Jurisprudence of Bangladesh

To accommodate any criminal legal doctrine in a national law, before exploring it in the international criminal law, it is of prime importance to find its presence in that nation's criminal jurisprudence. The reason behind this is a person cannot be made criminally liable for an act that was not punishable during the occurrence of that particular act, which is the underlying notion of principle of legality. This is also one of the fundamental rights under the Constitution of Bangladesh, which states that, 'No person shall be convicted of any offence except for violation of a law in force at the time of the commission of the act charged as an offence ...'[58]. Hence, if the criminal jurisprudence, that are applicable in Bangladesh, did not have a consistent practice of the doctrine of joint criminal enterprise, then JCE could not have been incorporated in any national laws of the country. Moreover, the doctrine of JCE also has to be recognized in the national laws of Bangladesh, so that the doctrine is 'foreseeable and accessible to the accused'.[59] Therefore, it is crucial to explore the doctrine of JCE in the criminal jurisprudence of Bangladesh that existed until 1971.[60]

The criminal jurisprudence of the area surrounding Bangladesh is enshrined in the *Penal Code* 1860. And Section 34 of this *Penal Code* provides the principle of joint liability for doing a criminal act.[61] The section asserts that, 'When a criminal act is done by several persons in furtherance of the common intention of all, each of such persons is liable for that act in the same manner as if it were done by him alone'. This provision does not create a separate crime; rather it merely enunciates a principle of joint liability for criminal offence.[62] Moreover, this liability under section 34 consists of three elements: i) a criminal act has been done by several persons, ii) all the participants intended that the criminal act should be done and iii) the criminal act has been done in furtherance of common intention shared by all of the offenders.[63]

---

[58] Article 35(1), Constitution of the Peoples' Republic of Bangladesh, 1972.

[59] *See* Luke Marsh, and Micheal Ramsden, "Joint Criminal Enterprise: Cambodia's Reply to *Tadić*", International Criminal Law Review, Vol. 11, No. 1, 2011, pp. 137-154, 145.

[60] Here the criminal jurisprudence of Bangladesh includes reported cases of *Penal Code* 1860. The year 1860 suggests that the criminal law of the Indian subcontinent was governed by the Penal Code. Therefore, whatever development JCE has undergone in this region came about through reported cases under this law.

[61] Moh. Anacharauddina Sikder, *Commentary on the Code of Criminal Procedure, Act V of 1898* (as amended up to date), published by M. Tanveer Faysal, Dhaka, 2000, 11.

[62] *Ibid.*, 12; AIR 1965 SC 264.

[63] *Id;* AIR 1965 SC 257.

Therefore what is required is a plurality of persons all having a common intention. Here common intention means, 'a pre-arranged plan and to convict the accused of an offence applying the section, it should be proved that the criminal act was done in concert pursuant to the pre-arranged plan'.[64] The basis of common intention is prior concert or pre-arranged plan.[65] Thus, when there is an intention to commit a crime that has been actually committed, each accused would be convicted if he shared that common intention. However, it does not always need to be formulated before the commencement of the crime; it may develop at the scene of the crime spontaneously.[66] Nonetheless, it has to be inferred from the conduct of the accused and circumstances of the case.[67]

Furthermore, besides sharing common intention, the most crucial test of applicability of this principle of joint liability under section 34 is the phrase 'in furtherance of common intention'. In the case of *Mahbub Shah*[68] Privy Council observed that:

> … [t]o convict an accused person applying section 34 of the Penal Code it must be proved that a criminal act was done in concert pursuant to the pre-arranged plan and that there should be direct evidence to prove common intention or there must be material to infer from the relevant circumstances that there was such common intention.[69]

Another primary element of this joint liability is, 'all accused must participate in the act in some way or other'.[70] It means that, everyone sharing the common intention has to do something to fulfill the common criminal plan. This section applies to cases where several persons both intend to do and actually do an act.[71] Thus, to be held liable under this section, the accused has to participate significantly in the commission of the crime. This significant participation does not mean that the accused has to do the ultimate crime. The criminal act can be done by any one of the participants. In this regard M. Ansar Uddin Sikder opined, 'criminal sharing, over or covert by active presence or by distant direction, making out a certain measure of jointness in

---

64 AIR 1945 PC 118.

65 *Hethubha vs. State of Gujrat,* (1971) 2 SCJ 635; AIR 1970 SC 1266.

66 M. Ansar Uddin Sikder, *Commentary on the Code of Criminal Procedure, Act V of* 1898 (as amended up to date), published by M. Tanveer Faysal, Dhaka, 2000, 17.

67 *Id.*

68 49 CWEN (PC) 678

69 *Id. See Kabul vs. The State,* 40 DLR 216.

70 AIR 1956 All 245.

71 AIR 1949 All 211, 1954 CrLJ 752; 1966 CrLJ 727.

the commission of the act is the essence of section 34'.[72] Therefore, from these above discussions it becomes apparent that the rationale of joint criminal enterprise in its basic form is firmly established in the criminal jurisprudence of Bangladesh till 1971.

However, it may be questioned that since the provision of joint liability already exists in the *Penal Code* 1860, thus does its application becomes restricted in the *International Crimes (Tribunals) Act,* 1973 under Article 35 (1) of the *Constitution of Bangladesh*? In this regard reference can be sought from the *Bangladesh vs. Sk. Hasina Wazed*[73] case where it was observed that, 'Where no new offence on past conduct is created ... Article 35(1) is not attracted merely because a new forum for trial of an existing offence is created'[74]. Therefore, the principle of joint liability can be applicable in the *ICT Act,* 1973 since it exists in the criminal jurisprudence of Bangladesh and its application is not restricted by the prohibition against *ex post facto law* enshrined in Article 35(1) of the Constitution.

4. SEEKING THE DOCTRINE IN THE PRACTICES OF INTERNATIONAL CRIMINAL LAW TILL 1971

In order to find the legal foundations of JCE in the arena of international criminal law prevailing in 1971, it is essential to look through the post–World War II legislations and cases. According to Ciara Damgaard, 'the origin of JCE doctrine can be found in the events surrounding the end of World War II'.[75] Moreover, the doctrine had been given 'customary international law' status in the *Tadić case* and later on in many other cases under international ad-hoc tribunals and courts.[76] In fact it is said that the three kinds of JCE are

[72] M. Ansar Uddin Sikder, 2000, 12, *op. cit.*

[73] *Bangladesh vs. Sk. Hasina Wazed,* (2008) 60 DLR (AD) 90.

[74] *Id.*

[75] Michael. P. Scharf, "Joint Criminal Enterprise, the Nuremberg Precedent, and the Concept of "Grotian Moment"", in *Accountability for Collective Wrongdoing,* edited by Isaacs T. and Vernon R., Cambridge University Press, New York, 2011, pp. 119-139, 137; quoting Ciara Damgaard, *Individual Criminal Responsibility for Core International Crimes,* Springer, New York, 2008, pp. 132, 235.

[76] *Prosecutor vs. Dusko Tadic,* July 15, 1999, para. 220, *op. cit.*; *See* also *The Prosecutor v. Milan Martic,* Appeals Chamber, International Criminal Tribunal for the Former Yugoslavia, IT-95-11-A, October 8, 2008, para. 80-81; *The Prosecutor v. Emmanuel Rukundo,* Trial Chamber, International Criminal Tribunal for Rwanda, ICTR-2001-70-T, February 27, 2009, para. 23; *Prosecutor v Milutinovic, Sainovic and Ojdanic,* Decision on Dragoljub Ojdanic Motion Challenging Jurisdiction – Joint Criminal Enterprise, Trail Chamber, International Criminal tribunal for the Former Yugoslavia, IT-99- 37-AR72, May 21, 2003, para 26. Since then other *ad-hoc* tribunals, i.e. ICTR, SCSL, Special Panel for Serious Crimes of East Timor, Iraqi High Tribunal have adopted this observation with out any further examination. However, The Extraordinary Chambers in the Courts of Cambodia is in one hand affirmative

also well settled in customary international law.[77] However, the customary status of this doctrine is not the concern of this paper and neither would it pursue on the much-debated topic of whether or not JCE exists in customary international law. Rather this section of this paper intends to look into the practices of international courts and tribunals that deal with similar international crimes to observe whether they have applied the doctrine of JCE or not.

The notion of JCE can be traced back from international legal instruments and international, national judicial decisions from the post-World War II period.[78] The conception of this doctrine can be found in three major post-World War II instruments: *The Charter of the International Military Tribunal at Nuremberg,* 1945 (IMT)*; Control Council. Law No. 10,* 1945; *Charter of the International Military Tribunal for the Far East,* 1946. Article 6 of the *Nuremberg Charter* asserts that:

> [t]hose who participated in the formulation of a Common Plan or Conspiracy to commit crimes against peace, war crimes, or crimes against humanity are responsible for all acts performed by any persons in the execution of such plan.

In the same way Article II (2) of *Control Council. Law No. 10* provides: 'Any person ... is deemed to have committed a crime ... if he was connected with plans or enterprises involving its commission'. The *Tokyo Charter* also held a similar view regarding criminalization based on common plan or purpose.[79] Therefore, two scopes of liabilities can be identified from these provisions: i) responsibilities for participating in a criminal plan, whether or not executed and ii) criminal liability for acts committed by any other participants in the execution of the criminal plan.[80] Thus the Trial Chamber of *Kupreškic*[81] observed that, the four Occupying Powers around 1945 adopted similar legislative instruments to try international crimes. It reflects intentions of the great powers of the world on the law applicable to international crimes, which

---

with *Tadić's* finding, but on other hand did not find sufficient evidence of consistent state practice or opinio juris at the relevant time. See Decision on the Appeals against the Co-Investigative Judges Order on Joint Criminal Enterprise *(JCE),* ECCC Pre-Trial Chamber, 002/19-09-2007-ECCC/OCIJ, May 20, 2010, para. 77.

[77] *Ieng Sary* Case, Co-Prosecutors' Supplementary Observations on Joint Criminal Enterprise, 002/19-09-2007-ECCC/OCIJ, December 31, 2008, para. 9.

[78] *Prosecutor vs. Milomir Stakić,* Appeals Chamber, International Criminal Tribunal for the former Yugoslavia, IT-97-24-A, Judgment, March 22, 2006, para. 62.

[79] Article 5, Charter of the International Military Tribunal for the Far East, 1946.

[80] *Co-Prosecutors vs. KAING Guek Eav alias "DUCH",* Octobor 27, 2008, para. 37, *op. cit.*

[81] *Prosecutor vs. Zoran Kupreškic et al.,* Trial Chamber, International Criminal Tribunal for the Former Yugoslavia, IT-95-16-A, Judgment, January 14, 2000.

signifies the fact that during that time states of the world wanted to apply this notion of JCE in trials of crimes of international nature.

Now, the paper will be looking at the applications of three forms of JCE in Nuremberg, Tokyo and other national case laws through their *factual matrix and judicial dictum*[82]. In the cases referred below, this paper will be demonstrating the basic form of JCE, where several persons share a common criminal intent and in execution of that common plan crimes are committed irrespective of the fact that not all of them were physical perpetrators of the crimes. Existence of JCE I can be found in the *Almelo* case[83]. In this case three Germans were convicted for murder of a British pilot and a Dutch civilian.[84] In the British Military Court it was observed that:

> If people were all present together at the same time, taking part in a common enterprise which was unlawful, each one in their own way assisting the common purpose of all, they were all equally guilty in law.[85]

After some time, during 1946 the application of common purpose doctrine was again seen in the *Hoelzer*[86] case, where Germans were convicted for executing a Canadian prisoner of war without trial.[87] In this case the Judge Advocate observed that:

> [t]he accused knew the purpose was to kill this airman, then, as the Court is well aware, persons together taking part in a common enterprise which is unlawful, each in their own way assisting the common purpose of all, then they are all equally guilty in point of law.[88]

From this observation, a rationale of JCE can be derived: when several person take part in a common criminal plan of an enterprise, then it is not necessary for each of them to take part in every step of the commencement of the crime, rather they may do different things to execute the ultimate purpose and still be equally liable for the crime committed. On the same year in the *Jepsen* case, the Judge Advocate of British Military Court convicted accused on the same principle of common purpose, by observing that:

---

[82] Luke Marsh, and Micheal Ramsden, 2011, 146, *op. cit.*

[83] *Trial of Otto Sandrock and three others,* British Military Court for the Trial of War Criminals, November 24, 1945, UNWCC, Vol. 1.

[84] *Ibid.,* pp. 35, 43.

[85] *Ibid.,* 43.

[86] *Hoelzer et al.,* Canadian Military Court, Aurich, Germany, March 25 - April 6, 1946, Record of Proceedings, Vol. I.

[87] *Ibid.,* pp. 341, 347, 349.

[88] *Id.*

> If Jepsen actively associated himself with and assisted the other guards in a wholesale slaughter, the act of every one of those persons became the act of all. There, the charged act was part of the common plan and Jepsen had played a direct role.[89]

The rationale derived from this case is: the common plan can be formulated at any time extemporaneously; it does not need to be formulated before commencement of the crime.

Subsequently, this doctrine of common purpose was further enforced in *Trial of Franz Schonfeld and Other*[90]. Moreover, in *Feurstein and Others (Ponzano case),* the level of participation by the accused of JCE was addressed. In that case the Judge Advocate observed that:

> A person can be concerned in the commission of a criminal offence, who, without being present at the place where the offence was committed, took such a part in the preparation for this offence as to further its object; in other words, he must be the cog in the wheel of events leading up to the result which in fact occurred. He can further that object not only by giving orders for a criminal offence to be committed, but he can further that object by a variety of other means.[91]

Therefore, the resulting interpretation from this observation is, to be a participant of JCE, the act of the accused has to be significant, which will help to obtain the ultimate purpose of the common plan. In the same case the requirement of 'guilty knowledge' for JCE I, was pointed out[92], which demonstrated that when the accused of JCE takes part in a common enterprise, he must know the intended purpose of it.[93] Moreover, in the *Einsatzgruppen* case[94], under the *Control Council. Law No. 10,* the Prosecution submitted that the provision of common purpose under Article II (2) is consistent with 'recognized principles common to all civilized legal system' and the

---

[89] *Trial of Gustav Alred Jepsen and others,* British Military Court, Proceedings of War Crimes Trials held at Luneberg, Germany, August 13-24, 1946.

[90] *Trial of Franz Schonfeld and others,* British Military Court, June 26, 1946, UNWCC, Vol. XI.

[91] *Feurstein and Others (Ponzano Case),* British Military Court sitting at Hamburg, Germany, Judgment, August 24, 1948, (on file in the Public Record Office, Kew Gardens, London, file WO 235/525), reproduced in *Journal of International Criminal Justice,* Vol. 5, No. 1, 2007, pp. 238-240, 239.

[92] *Ibid.,* pp. 239, 240.

[93] *Prosecutor vs. Dusko Tadic,* July 15, 1999, para. 199, *op. cit.*

[94] *The United States of America v. Otto Ohlendorf, et al.* (The *Einsatzgruppen* Case), Military Tribunal II, Case No. 9, Judgment, April 10, 1948, in *Trials of War Criminals before the Nuremberg Military Tribunals under Control Council Law* No. 10, Vol. IV.

participants of common criminal plan are all equally responsible for the crime as principal.[95] In consideration of this argument the tribunal found the accused guilty.[96]

Now the systematic form of JCE, which will be assessed through cases on concentration or detention camps. This form of JCE requires a systematic structure where the common plan is executed at different levels of the system. In this regard the first case is *Belsen* case[97] where the requirements for JCE II were chalked out: i) knowledge by the accused that a system of ill treatment is in force and ii) he participated in the course of conduct to further the system of ill treatment.[98] Similarly in the *Dachau Concentration Camp*[99] and *Mauthausen Concentration Camp*[100] cases, the Trial Chambers found the accused guilty for their participation in a system of ill treatment with knowledge of the criminality of the system and their acts in furtherance of that common plan of ill treatment.

At this instant, the paper will explore the application of JCE III in international courts and tribunals till 1971. This extended form of JCE deals with foreseeable crimes that occur in furtherance of a common criminal plan, which is outside the scope of that common plan but was a reasonable and foreseeable consequence of that plan, and the accused had nonetheless taken the risk of executing that common plan. In this regard reference can be drawn from the *Essen Lynching* case[101], where seven Germans were convicted of murder of three British prisoners of war.[102] Here the Captain loudly ordered his subordinates to escort the POWs and not to do anything if the mob tried to molest them. Consequent to this instigation the mob subsequently killed them out of extreme molestation. Thus the Captain was found guilty because he knowingly took the risk that such instigation might cause the death of those POWs.[103] Also in *Borkum Island* case[104] US Military Court convicted the

---

[95] *Ibid.*, pp. 369, 372.

[96] *Ibid.*, pp. 411, 578, 584.

[97] *Trial of Josef Kramer and 44 Others (The Belsen Trial)*, British Military Court, Luneberg, Case No. 10, September 17 – November 17, 1945, in *United National War Crimes Commission, Law Reports of trials of War Criminals*, Vol. II, 1947, 1.

[98] *Ibid.*, pp. 120-121.

[99] *The Trial of Martin Gottfried Weiss and thirty-nine others (The Dachau Concentration Camp Trial)*, General Military Government Court of the United States Zone, December 13, 1945, UNWCC, Vol. XI.

[100] *Mauthausen Concentration Camp case*, General Military Government Court of the U.S. Zone, Dachau, Germany, March 29 – May 13, 1946, in The United Nations War Crimes Commission, Law Reports of Trials of War Criminals, Vol. XI, 15.

[101] *Trial of Erich Heyer and Six Others*, British Military Court for the Trial of War Criminals, Essen, Case No. 8, December 18-19 and 21-22, 1945, in The United Nations War Crimes Commission, Law Reports of Trials of War Criminals, Vol. I, 1947, 88.

[102] *Ibid.*, pp. 88-89.

[103] *Id.*

[104] *Borkum Island* case, *See Prosecutor vs. Dusko Tadic*, July 15, 1999, para 210-213, *op. cit.*

Mayor of Borkum and some German men for assaulting and killing of seven U.S. men.[105]

The principles of JCE III have also been drawn from some cases under Italian Courts established after World War II for trials of war criminals.[106] It is important to note that, Italy took a similar approach like Nuremberg to try their accused. In *D'Ottavio and Others*[107], the Italian Court of Cassation opined that:

> [f]or a participant to be held liable for crimes other than the one intended, there had to be a causation nexus—which is not only objective but also psychological—between the fact committed and willed by all participants and the different fact committed by one of the participants.[108]

In this way, the court has upheld the main rationale of JCE III, which is: 'cause of a cause, is also the cause of the thing caused'[109], i.e. whenever a crime outside the scope of a planned crime happens, then whoever knowingly took the risk of committing the latter crime will be responsible for the former crime, whether or not he intended to commit the crime. However, these instances of vague application of the extended version of JCE do not prove its existence in the post-World War II jurisprudence. This is because there is no indication in these cases that the prosecutor relied on the concept of common design or common purpose. [110] Moreover, in international criminal jurisprudence, the extended version of JCE is a much-debated topic as it contradicts with several basic principles of justice.

Its extended nature is also a reason of fear that the theory of JCE III could be used to criminate those individuals who should not be held responsible under widely accepted limits of criminal law.[111] This is because its wide limit would take it to a point where mere membership in a group or association would become a criminal activity. In this regard Professor Harmen van der Wilt has a different way of thinking. According to him, instead of moulding

---

[105] Luke Marsh, and Micheal Ramsden, 2011, 149, *op. cit.*

[106] *Co-Prosecutors vs. KAING Guek Eav alias "DUCH"*, 2008, para. 53, *op. cit.*

[107] *D'Ottavio and Others Case,* Italian Court of Cassation, Criminal Section I, Case No. 270, Judgment, March 12, 1947, (Central Public Record Office, Rome), reprinted in *Journal of International Criminal Justice,* Vol. 5, No. 1, 2007, pp. 232-234.

[108] *Ibid.,* 232-233; similar approach of convicting criminals based on this extended responsibility was taken in other Italian cases. See *Aratano and Others* case, *Berardi case*, and *Mannelli and Others* case in the Italian Court of Cassation

[109] *Id.*

[110] Luke Marsh and Micheal Ramsden, 2011, 149, *op. cit.*

[111] Katrina Gustafson, "The Requirement of an 'Express Agreement' for Joint Criminal Enterprise Liability", Journal of International Criminal Justice, Vol. 5, 2007, pp. 134-158, 140.

the legal concept of JCE III to go along with the principles of justice, we should realize some better responsibility theory to tackle state bureaucracy and large organizations that engage in international crimes.[112]

Therefore, it is evident that in post-World War II era the basic and systematic JCE had strong existence, on the other hand extended form of JCE's existence is questionable. Here it is essential to note that the *ICT Act* 1973 is in line with those legal instruments, which were associated with post-World War II cases, since the said Act followed the principles of Nuremberg, Yamashita and Tokyo trials. Thus, as international crimes were integrally related to all these legal instruments, there would be no harm to apply the uncontroversial notion of JCE, developed till 1971, in the *ICT Act* 1973.

5. Exploring Applicability of the Doctrine in the International Crimes (Tribunals) Act 1973

The purpose, objective and language of the *International Crimes (Tribunals) Act,* 1973 has to be explored exhaustively to unearth the possibility of accommodating joint criminal enterprise in the Act. This Act of 1973 was an initiative of the Government of Bangladesh to prosecute heinous crimes committed during the 1971 Liberation War. It was a first of its kind, where the Parliament of Bangladesh enacted a domestic law by incorporating international crimes and norms of international justice.[113] In addition to that, the principles enumerated in Nuremberg, Tokyo and Yamachita trials were also followed.[114] As a result, the norms, principles and practices of those tribunals can be accommodated in the *ICT Act.* Moreover, the basic principle of JCE is also an established practice under the name of joint liability in the criminal jurisprudence of Bangladesh till 1971. Thus, the notion of JCE has scope in the *ICT Act,* because it was an established principle of criminal liability, under the criminal jurisprudence of Bangladesh, and in the international courts and tribunals dealing with crimes of similar nature during 1971.

Moreover, for the purpose of exploring the scope of JCE in this Act, the extent of criminal responsibility for individuals has to be determined. The preamble to the Act provides its scope regarding criminal accountability by enumerating that; the persons responsible for 'genocide, war crimes, crimes against humanity, and other crimes under international law' would be

---

[112] Harmen van der Wilt, "Joint Criminal Enterprise: Possibilities and Limitations", Journal of International Criminal Justice,Vol. 5, 2007, pp. 91-108, 92.

[113] Mr. Serajul Huq in Parliamentary Debates, *op. cit.*

[114] *Id.*

detained, prosecuted and punished.[115] Here by only mentioning 'persons' the scope of this Act is kept broad. Further, section 3 (1) of the *ICT Act* elaborates the types of persons on whom the tribunal will have jurisdiction. The section provides that:

> A Tribunal shall have power to try and punish any individual or group of individuals, or any member of any armed, defence or auxiliary forces, irrespective of his nationality, who commits or has committed, in the territory of Bangladesh, whether before or after the commencement of this Act, any of the crimes mentioned in sub-section 2.[116]

Here by the phrase 'any individual or group of individuals' the Act gets the opportunity to try every person responsible behind committing a crime, including those who did not participate in physical perpetration of a crime. And by stating 'any member of armed, defence or auxiliary forces', it also suggests its jurisdiction upon those who belongs to a systematic organized group. It is important to note here that, this systematic organized group is crucial for systematic JCE.[117] Thus, this provision provides for individual criminal responsibility on all those persons who are responsible in some way or other for committing a crime under this Act.

Furthermore, section 3 (1) of the Act also enumerates the level of participation of the concerned persons to be tried by the Tribunal(s), using the phrase 'commits or has committed'. Here the paper argues that by this mentioned phrase, the *ICT Act* not only covers physical perpetration but also covers other types of perpetration of crimes committed in realization of common purpose or common plan. The paper finds support for this contention from reading section 3(1) along with section 3(2). This is because; 'planning, preparation, initiation or waging of a war of aggression' in violation of international laws is a crime;[118] and the 'attempt, abetment or conspiracy to commit any crime' is also a crime,[119] under this said Act. Thus, it is apparent from the language of section 3 (1) as well from the definition of crimes given in section 3 (2) that the phrase 'commits or has committed' does not only mean those individuals who are direct perpetrators of crimes but also means those who are parties to a common criminal plan and had taken substantial part in furtherance of that common intention.

---

[115] Preamble to the International Crimes (Tribunals) Act, 1973.

[116] Section 3 (1), International Crimes (Tribunals) Act, 1973.

[117] This is because, for being liable under systematic JCE, the accused has to be a participant of a system of ill treatment, i.e. concentration camp or detention camp, which usually belongs under organized military or auxiliary group.

[118] Section 3 (2) (b), International Crimes (Tribunals) Act, 1973.

[119] *Ibid.*, section 3 (2) (g).

This paper attained additional hold on the abovementioned submission in the purpose and object of the concerned Act. In the Parliamentary Debate on *International Crimes (Tribunals) Bill,* 1973, Mr. Serajul Huq stated that, this law 'is for clearing the conscience of humanity at large'.[120] He further stated that, 'the *Summum Bonum* of this law is justice for all and at all cost'.[121] Therefore, the purpose of this Act is to try all those responsible persons behind committing those grievous crimes, either directly or indirectly. This purpose was also upheld through the speech given by Sri Monoronjon Dhor[122] in the Parliamentary Debate, where he stated that:

> Those who have attacked humanity, human civilization, human peace and tranquility, world peace, what we understand as our values and principles of humanity, and those who have campaigned against religious faith are enemies of human civilization and will be tried under this Act.[123]

Therefore, from these above statements, it become clear that this Act has jurisdiction to try all those persons who participated in the commission of serious crimes under international law, irrespective of their level of participation.

Now, by referring to the Parliamentary Debates a controversy regarding the scope of the Act has been created, where it is contended that the Act was made only for the purpose of trying 195 war criminals that were prisoners of war, but not to try any citizens of Bangladesh. In order to get a clear view on the extent of the Act in concern, this controversy needs to be addressed. This paper does not contend that, the trial of 195 persons was not the concern of the Act. Rather it asserts the fact that, although the trials of those 195 persons under this Act is mentioned in the Parliamentary Debates,[124] these trials were not the only purpose of the Act and the purpose of the Act has been kept open to try everyone including those who are citizens of Bangladesh. This was confirmed in Mr. Serajul Huq's speech:

> We have tried to make this law not only for those 195 persons who are prisoners of war, but also for our own armed forces

---

[120] Mr. Serajul Huq in Parliamentary Debates, *op. cit.*
[121] *Ibid.*, 2357.
[122] The Minister of Law, Justice and Parliamentary Affairs during 1973.
[123] Sri Monoronjon Dhor in Parliamentary Debates on International Crimes (Tribunals) Bill, 1973, Vol. 2, No. 37, 2359; Translated by the Author for the purpose of this paper.
[124] Mr. Serajul Huq in Parliamentary Debates, 2356, *op. cit.*

> and our own people, having regard to the principles of Geneva Convention. ...[125]

Therefore, the argument that this law is only for those 195 Pakistani prisoners of war and not for any Bangladeshi nationals is unsubstantiated. Moreover, in the Parliamentary Debates during 1973 it was called upon several times to add the types of persons specifically, on whom the tribunal(s) would have jurisdiction, in section 3 (1) of the Act. But this specification was never incorporated into the Act. Thus its limit was kept as wide as possible allowing for it try personalities beyond the 195 POWs, such as the collaborators of Pakistan Army, who were Bangladeshi nationals. This purpose can be understood form the language of the said section, which used the phrase 'irrespective of his nationality'. These words do not exclude those who are nationals of Bangladesh, but they include those as well who are not nationals of this country. Therefore, it can be safely contended that this Act has jurisdiction over collaborators of Pakistan Army during 1971, who are nationals of Bangladesh.

Now after specifying the purpose of the Act, this paper would go back to the language of section 4. The scope of the doctrine of JCE is further supported by section 4 (1) of the *ICT Act*, which enunciates that, 'When any crime as specified in section 3 is committed by several persons, each of such person is liable for that crime on the same manner as if it were done by him alone'. Thus by this provision the *ICT Act* asserts the principle of joint liability for committing a crime. Therefore, the principles of basic form of JCE can be safely accommodated in the *ICT Act.* Here it is important to note that, as systematic form of JCE is not explicitly present in the criminal jurisprudence of Bangladesh, the paper does not confirm its accommodation in the Act, because of the distinct nature of international crimes and its presence in dealing with similar crimes in post-World War II international courts and tribunals. Systematic form of JCE requires an organized system of ill treatment, which is a rare scenario in national crimes. On the other hand, this organized system of ill treatment is not at all rare in times of war, and it exists in concentration camps and detention camps.[126]

6. Conclusion

This paper has showed the resonance and scope of the doctrine of joint criminal enterprise in the *International Crimes (Tribunals) Act,* 1973. The Act

---

[125] Mr. Serajul Huq in Parliamentary Debates, *op. cit.*

[126] These kinds of detention camps were present during 1971 war, where Bangladeshi armed forces, who were injured or prisoners, were kept. Women and suspected persons were also kept in camps of enemy force.

accommodates this doctrine through its very purpose and language. In the process of searching for its scope, the paper found that the doctrine in the form of common intention liability was present before 1971 in the territory that we now call Bangladesh demonstrating the existence of JCE in the criminal jurisprudence of Bangladesh. Further, the paper showed that the notion of JCE under the heads of common purpose liability or common criminal plan or common design in its basic and systematic form was firmly practiced by the international tribunals and courts as well as some national courts trying international crimes in the post-World War II period. However, some vague applications of extended form of JCE were found in some post-World War II cases, but they did not suggest a contentious practice. Thus this paper does not advocate accommodation of extended form of JCE in the *ICT Act.*

As a result of these observations, this paper submits that the principle of JCE is in line with the 'principle of legality', because it existed at the time when the crimes were committed in 1971. This criminal liability was also foreseeable to the accused[127], since it existed in the criminal jurisprudence, which established the criminal law of Bangladesh, during 1971. Here also this paper did not find any resonance of extended JCE in the national jurisprudence of Bangladesh. Although, systematic form of JCE could not be found as well, the paper argues that this form of JCE requires the situation of war, which cannot exist in national law. But the *ICT Act*, 1973 has room for systematic JCE, thus the paper affirms its accommodation as well in the Act besides basic form of JCE.

The Bangladesh justice system, after a long 40 years of Independence, is on the verge of trying persons alleged to have committed core international crimes during 1971. The whole nation that wants justice for those brutal crimes is looking towards the Tribunals, and to be specific, to the Office of the Chief Prosecutor. The application of this doctrine of JCE would definitely facilitate the justice process that is going on under the *ICT Act*, 1973. By imposing equal liability on perpetrators of crimes who did not participate physically, but who facilitated substantially to the commission of crime, the doctrine would be applicable to all crimes committed during 1971 making it ideal to address the mass crimes committed during the war.

The International Crimes Tribunals of Bangladesh constituted under the concerned Act are purely domestic in nature. They are not bound by the international norms and standards, unless some resemblance is found between the national and international norms and practices. However, this paper is not trying to impose any international standard of criminal liability, which is alien to the criminal jurisprudence of Bangladesh; rather it has traced the existence of this doctrine in the legal system of Bangladesh. Therefore, it is the

---

[127] Which is a pre-requisite to establish *principle of legality*.

prerogative of the tribunal(s), to be specific the judges of the tribunal to apply it in such way so that the doctrine of joint criminal enterprise retains its national essence.

Ukrainian Sovereignty and Territorial Integrity – Has it Been Breached?

Alexander Gilder[1]

In November 2013 the Euromaidan protests swept Kiev and brought violence to the streets. President Yanukovyk had chosen closer economic ties to the Russian Federation over the European Union and in February he was ousted and an acting-President appointed by Ukrainian Parliament. The crisis escalated when unmarked forces seized the Crimean peninsula and penned Ukrainian forces into their bases. Furthermore, Eastern Ukraine saw increased pro-Russian protests against the Government and in the subsequent twelve months the rebel groups that seized control have attempted to create break away from Ukraine. The rebel groups have been supported by Russia by provisions of weapons, armour and logistics but the full extent of Russia's involvement is unclear. This article locates the breaches of international law with regards to Russia's actions in Ukraine and addresses the extent to which the sovereignty of Ukraine has been violated. The use of force and potential acts of aggression are examined and the right to self-determination of the Ukrainian people.

Keywords: International Law, Ukraine Crisis, Russia, Use of Force, Sovereignty, Self-Determination

1. Introduction

Civil unrest had been on going for months when President Yanukovych was ousted to Russia in February 2014. Russian troops began to seize control of the Crimean peninsula, Ukrainian territory since 1954, and Crimea was

[1] LLB, University of Lincoln; LLM candidate, Public International Law & Human Rights, Utrecht University.

subjugated from the Ukrainian mainland.[2] Shortly after the Crimean crisis, fighting broke out in Eastern Ukraine that has resulted in attempts by rebel groups, allegedly supplied by Russia, to gain independence from Ukraine.[3] The legal status of Ukraine as a state is not in doubt and the international community have condemned the breaches of the sovereignty and territorial integrity of Ukraine. The crisis bears some resemblance to that of the Georgian conflict in 2008.[4] Similarly in this crisis, Russia justified its actions by claiming intervention by invitation and protection of its nationals.

It is regarded by Jean-Claude Juncker that, "What the Russian leadership has done in Crimea is in clear contravention of international law."[5] With that statement in mind, firstly, the concepts and rights of sovereignty will be analysed. Secondly, the specific obligations of Russia under various treaties that enshrine cooperation in that sovereignty must be examined. Thirdly, Russia has arguably used force in contravention of international law and has suggested a number of defences as reasoning for its actions. Lastly, what role does self-determination have in those actions?

2. Relevant International Law and Principles

As is the situation with many international crises the legal issues blend with political considerations but there remains underlying legal principles, which must be adhered to. In the words of President Putin himself, "[we] believe that preserving law and order in today's complex and turbulent world is one of the few ways to keep international relations from sliding into chaos. The law is still the law, and we must follow it whether we like it or not."[6] Firstly, all states are sovereign and equal which comes from the maxim *par in parem non habet imperium* that stipulates one sovereign power cannot exercise jurisdiction over another.[7] Ukraine has sovereignty over its territory, which is the "capacity as the entity entitled to exercise control over its territory and its

---

[2] 'Nato accuses Russia of violating Ukraine sovereignty' (BBC News, 29 August 2014) <http://www.bbc.co.uk/news/world-europe-28984241> accessed 2 February 2015.

[3] *Ibid.*

[4] Alexander Lott, 'The Tagliavini Report Revisited: Jus ad Bellum and the Legality of the Russian Intervention in Georgia' [2012] Utrecht Journal of International and European Law, 28 (74) 2-21.

[5] Christian Ignatzi, 'Crimea: A breach of international law' (Deutsche Welle, 8 March 2014) < http://dw.de/p/1BMEj> accessed 2 February 2015.

[6] Kristin Hausler, Robert McCorquodale, 'Ukraine Insta-Symposium: Crimea, Ukraine and Russia: Self-Determination, Intervention and International Law' (Opinio Juris, 10 March 2014) <http://opiniojuris.org/2014/03/10/ukraine-insta-symposium-crimea-ukraine-russia-self-determination-intervention-international-law/> accessed 2 February 2015.

[7] James Crawford, *Brownlie's Principles of International Law* (8th edn, OUP, 2012)245.

people."[8] Sovereign states have a wider obligation of non-intervention in the jurisdiction of other states and must adhere to treaties it has signed and customary law.[9] Russia and Ukraine have multiple treaties that were signed after the dissolution of the Soviet Union, the first of which is the Budapest Memorandum on Security Assurances.[10] It stipulates that Russia, the UK and the USA will respect the independence and sovereignty of Ukraine's borders.[11] The second treaty is the Treaty of Friendship, Cooperation, and Partnership between Ukraine and Russia.[12] Article 2 states they will have "respect for each other's territorial integrity, and confirm the inviolability of the borders existing between them." These treaties emphasise the sovereignty and independence of Ukraine, which had only been created in its current form a few years earlier. Due to the close alignment of the former Soviet Bloc the two countries signed the Agreement on the Presence of the Black Sea Fleet (BSFA).[13] The agreement arose from the fleet being divided between the two nations. Russia wished to keep its warm water port to access the Mediterranean but the prominent Ukrainian politician Chomovil foresaw the problem with allowing a Russian port on Ukrainian territory when he said, "to leave the Russian Black Sea Fleet [in Sevastopol] for 20 years is to force a pervasive and permanent atmosphere of agitation and strain not only in the Crimea, but in Ukraine."[14] The treaty notably instructs "Russian forces to respect the sovereignty and legislation of Ukraine and to refrain from interfering in its internal affairs; [and] Article 8(2), which restricts Russian forces to carrying out maneuvers and exercises within the areas agreed to by the Ukrainian authorities…"[15] The three key regional and international treaties provide the framework that solidify the status of Ukraine as a nation free to decide its own destiny and in which Russia's actions must be judged.

---

[8] *Ibid.,* 244.

[9] *Ibid.,* 245.

[10] Budapest Memorandum on Security Assurances (adopted 5 December 1994) UN Doc A/49/765

[11] *Ibid.,* Art. 1.

[12] Treaty on Friendship, Cooperation, and Partnership between Ukraine and the Russian Federation (adopted 31 May 1997).

[13] Agreement between Ukraine and the Russian Federation on the Status and Conditions of Presence of the Black Sea Fleet of the Russian Federation in the Territory of Ukraine (adopted 28 May 1997).

[14] Anka Feldhusen, 'Geography and the Boundaries of Confidence: The "Russian Factor" in Ukrainian Foreign Policy' [1999] 23 Fletcher F. World Aff., 126.

[15] Aurel Sari, 'Ukraine Insta-Symposium: When does the Breach of a Status of Forces Agreement amount to an Act of Aggression? The Case of Ukraine and the Black Sea Fleet SOFA' (Opinio Juris, 6 March 2014) < http://opiniojuris.org/2014/03/06/ukraine-insta-symposium-breach-status-forces-agreement-amount-act-aggression-case-ukraine-black-sea-fleet-sofa/> accessed 2 February 2015.

Russia has undoubtedly used a level of aggression and force in Ukraine through various methods. The prohibition on the use of force is in Art. 2(4) of the UN Charter which states, "All Members shall refrain in their international relations from the threat or use of force against the territorial integrity or political independence of any state, or in any other manner inconsistent with the Purposes of the United Nations."[16] Not using armed force is also customary law and if no defences to make the action legal can be successfully argued, the use of force is a violation of a rule of *jus cogens* and constitutes aggression. As members of the UN, Ukraine and Russia are both bound by these obligations. Under the 1974 Definition of Aggression, Art. 3 provides guidance which is important in the current crisis. Article 3(a) states aggression is the invasion or attack of one state on another; 3(e) prohibits troops stationed in another state to go beyond the agreement of their presence (for example, BSFA); and 3(g) prohibits the use of mercenaries to carry out acts of armed force against another state.[17] Article 3(g) is recognised in *Nicaragua v USA*[18] but the court found that "the concept of 'armed attack' [does not include] … assistance to rebels in the form of the provision of weapons or logistical or other support."[19] In this case the USA was found to have intervened in the affairs of Nicaragua by equipping and financing the rebel Contras, which in turn also violated Nicaragua's sovereignty.[20] That being said, for the USA to be held solely responsible the rebel groups had to be under the direct control of the USA, which was not the case. More problematic is the definition of an 'armed attack'. 'Armed attack' is important because, "State practice seems to reveal that 'governments have been virtually unanimous in rejecting any right to use force except in response to an armed attack'."[21] Furthermore the, "Chatham House Principles … take the view that '[a]n armed attack means any use of armed force, and does not need to cross some threshold of intensity'."[22] Chatham House are an influential, respected, think-tank, providing research on international current affairs. Following Chatham House and the 1974 Declaration, "a good case can indeed be made that their presence and conduct fits the archetypical example of aggression…"[23] Russia committed an armed attack in Crimea by stationing its troops outside the

---

[16] Charter of the United Nations (adopted 24 October 1945) Art. 2(4).

[17] UN General Assembly, 'Definition of Aggression' (14 December 1974) UN Doc A/RES/29/3314.

[18] *Military and Paramilitary Activities in and against Nicaragua (Nicaragua v. United States of America)* [1986] ICJ Rep 14.

[19] *Ibid.,* [195].

[20] *Ibid.,* [111].

[21] Ahmed Khayre, 'Self-defence, intervention by invitation, or proxy war? The legality of the 2006 Ethiopian invasion of Somalia' [2014] A.J.I.C.L. 22(2),215.

[22] David Kretzmer, 'The inherent right to self-defence and proportionality in jus ad bellum' [2013] E.J.I.L. 24(1),243.

[23] Sari (n 14).

agreed bases but presence of an attack by Russia in Eastern Ukraine is less clear due to the lack of evidence if the rebels also include serving Russian military.

3. The Russian Defences

Where does Russia fall in its use of force and can it defend those actions? The presence of illegal force is clear where Russian troops, even without insignia, violated the sovereignty of Ukraine by breaking the BSFA and committed an act of aggression in Crimea, clarified by Malcolm Shaw QC.[24] The difficulty arises when discussing the situation in Eastern Ukraine. The level of Russian cooperation and support in facilitating the Ukrainian rebels is unclear but at a minimum the provisions of weapons and logistics falls under *Nicaragua* and is a gross violation of Ukrainian sovereignty even if the support does not amount to the use of force by Russia. Furthermore, it can be submitted that, "if a third state military intervenes in such a situation [civil war], it is 'using military force to curtail the political independence of the State and therefore it is an action that contravenes article 2(4)'."[25] Considering the Eastern Ukraine crisis as civil war and the reported crossings of Russian troops and armoured units into Ukraine, if true, it seems clearer that the sovereignty and territorial integrity of Ukraine has been violated on both fronts and Ukraine can take countermeasures to combat the attack.[26]

Nevertheless, Russia has claimed defences in its use of force and these form the main legal argument. Defences recognised in international law are self-defence, invitation by the lawful government, humanitarian intervention and action permitted by the UN Security Council.[27] First claimed by Russia is self-defence under Article 51 which states, "Nothing in the present Charter shall impair the inherent right of individual or collective self-defence if an armed attack occurs against a Member of the United Nations."[28] This is valid until the Security Council takes its own measures to ensure international peace and any use of the defence must be immediately reported.[29] The defence has its origins in *The Caroline* where, "it has long been accepted that, for it to be invoked or justified, the necessity for action must be instant, overwhelming and leaving no choice of means and no moment for deliberation."[30] Furthermore, "For Russia to rely on self-defence though, it needs to

[24] Scott Appleton, 'Fighting for a better future' [2014] IBA Global Insight, Jun/Jul.
[25] Khayre (n 20)224.
[26] Lott (n 3)11
[27] Khayre (n 20)211.
[28] UN Charter (n 15) Art. 51.
[29] *Ibid.*
[30] United Nations Security Council, 2283rd Meeting (15 June 1981) UN Doc S/PV.2283 [148].

demonstrate that an armed attack has taken place against it or that such an attack is imminent, that its use of force was necessary to end or prevent the attack, and that the force used was proportionate to that need."[31] This concept of necessity and proportionality originates from the *Oil Platforms Case.*[32] For self-defence to be successfully used the military personnel in Crimea must have been subject to an attack by Ukraine and this simply "did not occur and cannot be invoked in order to justify the Russian resort to armed force."[33] Wisehart further concludes that Russia bears the burden of proof in this situation under the *Oil Platform Case* and must "show that Ukrainian acts against Russian military personnel are of such a gravity to constitute an 'armed attack'."[34] This is clearly not the case in Crimea since Russian troops, in violation of the BSFA, penned in Ukrainian bases and no attack by Ukraine is apparent. With regards to the stationing of troops on Ukrainian territory the case of *Re Karins*[35] may be mentioned to highlight that the stationing of Soviet troops in Latvia was an act of aggression. By going beyond the BSFA the troops committed acts of aggression and due to the fact there was not an apparent attack on Russian forces the aggression could not be argued to be in self-defence.

The second defence raised by Russia is the protection of nationals. The concept was first introduced in 1952 with regards to a state's own nationals in a second state where Sir Humphrey Waldock laid down three rules for intervention.[36] Russia claims it wishes to protect ethnic Russians, which implies some of the ethnic Russians will be both Ukrainian and Russian nationals. The Russian Duma stated this when the use of force was authorised.[37] Vladimir Putin claimed "his country's role in Ukraine [is] safeguarding ethnic Russians worried by lawlessness spreading east from the capital."[38] In addition, the Russian Foreign Minister said, "it was not in

---

[31] Ruma Mandal, 'Russia, Ukraine and International Law' (Chatham House, The Royal Institute of International Affairs, 7 March 2014) <https://www.chathamhouse.org/media/comment/view/198003#> accessed 2 February 2015.

[32] *Oil Platforms (Islamic Republic of Iran v. United States of America)* [2003] ICJ 4.

[33] Daniel Wisehart, 'The Crisis in Ukraine and the Prohibition of the Use of Force: A Legal Basis for Russia's Intervention?' (Blog of the European Journal of International Law, 4 March 2014) <www.ejiltalk.org/the-crisis-in-ukraine-and-the-prohibition-of-the-use-of-force-a-legal-basis-for-russias-intervention/> accessed 3 February 2015.

[34] Wisehart (n 32).

[35] *Re Kariņš and others v Parliament of Latvia and Cabinet of Ministers of Latvia* [2007] Case No. 2007-10-0102 (Latvian Constitutional Court) (OUP Ref. ILDC 884 (LV 2007)).

[36] Wisehart (n 32).

[37] Norwegian Helsinki Committee, 'Ukraine, Russia crisis: breached of international law and human rights issues' (*NHC Policy Paper No.1 2014*, 20 March 2014) < http://www.nhc.no/filestore/Publikasjoner/Policy_Paper/NHC_PolicyPaper_1_2014UkraineQA.pdf> accessed 2 February 2015, 4.

[38] Robert McMahon, 'Ukraine in Crisis' (Council on Foreign Relations, 25 August 2014) <http://www.cfr.org/ukraine/ukraine-crisis/p32540> accessed 2 February 2015.

Russia's interests for Ukraine to break up, but that Moscow wanted all citizens of the country to be given equal treatment by Kiev."[39] Under the 'responsibility to protect', "it is intended to permit (and even require) international action in the face of the most serious human rights abuses or international crimes, in cases where a state fails in its duty to protect its own citizens."[40] In 2001 the concept was expanded to include protection of another state's nationals and is said to be an emerging norm of international law.[41] It was suggested in the 2001 Report of the International Commission on Intervention and State Sovereignty[42] a state may act, "(a) when a particular state is clearly unwilling or unable to fulfil its responsibility to protect; (b) where a particular state is itself the perpetrator of crimes or atrocities; or (c) where people living outside a particular state are directly threatened by actions taking place there."[43] The Entebbe hostage incident in 1976 and the Russian invasion of Georgia in 2008 are cited as examples of state practice of protecting nationals but it must be shown the nationals were indeed in danger.[44] There is considerable dispute in academia with regards to protecting nationals mentioned by both Wisehart and Talmon.[45] It is argued the provisions are in place to protect civilians from crimes against humanity and to avoid situations where states must "stand idly by whilst millions of human beings are massacred just because in the Security Council a permanent member holds its protective hands over the culprit."[46] "However, no evidence shows that Russians have been under a real physical threat; there was no humanitarian or human rights crisis. Russia could in no way invoke a doctrine of humanitarian intervention in order to justify its intervention."[47] Russia cannot demonstrate that civil strife in the form of protests and the Ukrainian change of law regarding use of the Russian language amounted to a human rights crisis and therefore, the 'responsibility to protect' cannot be used as a defence for actions in Crimea. It is reported that in Eastern Ukraine the civilian population are being attacked and killed but reports on the

---

[39] Antonia Molloy, 'Ukraine crisis: Russia is deliberately 'violating the independence and sovereignty of Ukraine', says William Hague' (*The Independent*, 14 April 2014) < http://www.independent.co.uk/news/world/europe/ukraine-crisis-russia-is-deliberately-violating-the-independence-and-sovereignty-of-ukraine-says-william-hague-9259024.html> accessed 2 February 2015.

[40] Crawford (n 6), 755.

[41] *Ibid.*, 756.

[42] International Commission on Intervention and State Sovereignty, 'The Responsibility To Protect' (Report of the ICISS, December 2001) < http://responsibilitytoprotect.org/ICISS%20Report.pdf> accessed 13 February 2015.

[43] Crawford (n 6), 756.

[44] Wisehart (n 32); Lott (n 3).

[45] Wisehart (n 32); Ignatzi (n 4).

[46] Crawford (n 6), 757.

[47] Norwegian Helsinki Committee (n 36), 4.

responsibility of states and groups involved are unclear. Although Kotlyar claims the shooting in Eastern Ukraine is due to the Ukrainian military, another consideration is that the Ukrainian military are attempting to reclaim territory which is legally part of Ukraine and has been seized by rebels with the support of a foreign power.[48] To determine if a humanitarian crisis exists, and if Russia acted to create the crisis or alleviate it, will be a matter for debate within the Security Council and General Assembly of the UN.

Lastly, the third defence submitted by Russia is an invitation to intervene. Such a request would mean that Article 2(4) prohibition would not apply.[49] Russia claims, "[the] Prime Minister of Crimea, went to the President of Russia with a request for assistance to restore peace in Crimea. According to available information, the appeal was also supported by Mr. Yanukovych, whose removal from office, we believe, was illegal."[50] The argument over the status of Yanukovych roots from Putin claiming, "Yanukovych is still *de jure* President of Ukraine (even if *de facto* ousted)."[51] Two theories exist for the lawful use of invitation to intervene, one of which supports the acting-President at the time, Turchynov, and the second supports Russian claims of Yanukovych's legitimacy. Firstly, "Under the effective control theory, the sole authority entitled to speak on behalf of a state is the one which has permanent *de facto* control over that state's territory and population." The acting-President had *de facto* control of Ukraine as per his appointment by Ukrainian Parliament. Secondly, "Under the popular sovereignty theory the loss of effective control does not affect the continued legitimacy of a democratically elected (and unconstitutionally overthrown) government."[52] It can be evidenced by practice in 1979 that the international community has previously denied Russian use of a questionable invitation to intervene where the Prime Minister of Afghanistan, "crowned" by the Soviet Union, invited military intervention that was deemed illegal.[53] The acting-President must be granted legitimacy by the fact of his appointment by democratically elected MPs in a time of national emergency. As a result, the invitation of intervention by former President Yanukovych must be invalid.

---

[48] Todd Benjamin, 'Ukraine crisis' [2015] *IBA Global Insight*, Dec/Jan, 39.

[49] *Military and Paramilitary Activities in and against Nicaragua (Nicaragua v. United States of America)* [1986] ICJ Rep 14 [246].

[50] United Nations Security Council, 7124th Meeting (1 March 2014) UN Doc S/PV.7124, 5.

[51] Grigory Vaypan, '(Un)Invited Guests: The Validity of Russia's Argument on Intervention by Invitation' (*Cambridge Journal of International and Comparative Law*, 5 March 2014) <http://cjicl.org.uk/2014/03/05/uninvited-guests-validity-russias-argument-intervention-invitation/> accessed 3 February 2015.

[52] Vypan (n 50).

[53] Khayre (n 20), 228.

4. International Opinion

The international opinion on the Ukraine crisis is united under General Assembly Resolution 2625 which, "affirms its commitment to the sovereignty, political independence, unity and territorial integrity of Ukraine within its internationally recognized borders."[54] The Resolution specifically calls for states to refrain from using force to modify the borders of Ukraine.[55] Furthermore, the body that can make binding decisions is the UN Security Council that often has political constraints when tackling crises due to splits in the policies of the permanent members.[56] A proposed binding Resolution would have made any territorial gains by Russia illegal by use of force and declared the Crimean referendum as invalid.[57] Due to Russia's belief of the actions being legal they used their veto to prevent the Security Council taking measures to denounce the conflict. This prompted a strong response from the UK Ambassador among others, "Russia alone is prepared to violate international law, disregard the UN Charter, and tear up its bilateral treaties."[58] It is an unfortunate caveat of the UN Security Council to be denied the ability to take action because of the politics of diplomacy but as Sir Mark Lyall Grant correctly says, "This message will be heard well beyond the walls of this chamber."[59] The Secretary-General called for, "the full respect for and preservation of the independence, sovereignty and territorial integrity of Ukraine."[60]

The concerns of the international community are not only limited to the illegal use of force, the UN Ambassador for Jordan states, "There have been increasing numbers of crimes against citizens, including forced displacement, torture and forced labour, and the deprivation of the right of citizens to stability and security"[61], and "Ukrainian pilot Nadia Savchenko … was taken by separatists in mid-June. She is now being held — where? — in a prison in Voronezh, Russia."[62] The illegal detention of a Ukrainian pilot by Russia is an indication to what extent the rebels are being assisted and perhaps acting on

---

[54] United Nations General Assembly 'Declaration on Principles of International Law concerning Friendly Relations and Co-operation among States in accordance with the Charter of the United Nations' (24 October 1970) UN Doc A/RES/25/2625, 2.

[55] *Ibid.*

[56] Khayre (n 20), 219.

[57] United Nations Security Council, Draft Resolution (15 March 2014) UN Doc S/2014/189.

[58] United Nations Security Council, 7138th Meeting (15 March 2014) UN Doc S/PV.7138, 5 per Sir Mark Lyall Grant.

[59] *ibid.*, 5.

[60] UN Security Council (n 49), 2.

[61] United Nations Security Council, 7287th Meeting (24 October 2014) UN Doc S/PV.7287, 12.

[62] United Nations Security Council, 7219th Meeting (18 July 2014) UN Doc S/PV.7219., 6 per Ms. Power.

the orders of Russia. This cannot be allowed to continue and the root cause of this instability is the use of force by Russia to violate Ukrainian sovereignty.

Furthermore the Council of the European Union has joined the UN in denouncing the actions of Russia. They have stated, "Any unilateral military actions on the part of the Russian Federation in Ukraine under any pretext, including humanitarian, will be considered by the European Union as a blatant violation of international law."[63] In particular Russia are urged to sever their support of the rebels and withdraw its forces from the region.[64] The EU wishes to open dialogue between the parties and six months after the Council's conclusions a ceasefire was negotiated by Chancellor Merkel, unfortunately the Russian response to this ceasefire was increased military exercises and a rush to send armour over the border to Ukraine before the deadline.

5. The Right of Self-Determination

It must be examined if the peoples' exercise of self-determination harms the sovereignty of Ukraine. It is said that, "The importance of the principle of territorial integrity is a severe limitation to the exercise in practice of the right of self-determination, and has indeed in many instances outweighed any claim to self-determination."[65] On the other hand, it is stated in Article 1 of the ICCPR that, "All peoples have the right of self-determination."[66] Under the *Quebec* requirements a people are allowed self-determination where they are part of a colonial empire; where they are subject to alien subjugation, domination or exploitation; or where the people are denied the exercise of their rights within the state.[67] Dixon notes that it is unclear if the *Quebec* requirements reflect customary law[68] and more recently the right to self-determination has been recognised as an, "inalienable, permanent and unqualified right."[69] Nevertheless, Dixon argues for a balance to "be struck between protecting human rights of peoples and preserving the

[63] Council of the European Union, 'Council conclusions on Ukraine' (Press EN, Brussels, 15 August 2014) <http://www.europarl.europa.eu/meetdocs/2014_2019/documents/sede/dv/sede110914conclusionsukraine1508_/sede110914conclusionsukraine1508_en.pdf> accessed 11 February 2015, 1.

[64] *Ibid.*

[65] Laura Rees-Evans, 'Secession and the use of force in international law' [2008] C.S.L.R. 4(2),, 249.

[66] International Covenant on Civil and Political Rights (adopted 16 December 1966, entered into force 23 March 1976) 999 UNTS 171 (ICCPR).

[67] *ibid.*, 257; *Re Secession of Quebec* [1998] 2 S.C.R. 217.

[68] Martin Dixon, *International Law* (7th edn, OUP, 2013), 173.

[69] UN Human Rights Council, 43rd Meeting (26th March 2009) Resolution 10/20, 2.

fabric of international society."[70] Considering that viewpoint, Ukraine did not abuse the human rights of the people of Crimea and the referendum increased tensions perhaps harming the fabric of international society. Furthermore, European Parliament supports this view where, "It is recognized that the application of the principle of self-determination is possible only if the central government does not meet the requirements of the territory, which it wants, to give to this territory the territorial or national autonomy."[71] Kotlyar claims the people of Crimea were allowed self-determination from a government who wanted to repeal a law that allowed the Russian language to be used when speaking to Ukrainian authorities.[72] The Ukrainian government was not given the chance to meet the requirements of the territory before the Crimean people exercised self-determination. Tolstykh argues the sovereignty of Ukraine was not undermined by the Crimean referendum because the political forces in power had already undermined the constitution and that Ukraine had been divided into two smaller states, one which supported the Government from the coup and one which did not.[73] He also claims the military presence of Russian troops is not of concern because other referendums have occurred in that fashion.[74] This is contrasted by the conclusion of the EU that, "Plebiscite, held under the condition of the foreign occupation of the region, will not be recognized by the international community, and its results will be viewed as legally void."[75] The Ukraine has responded to the statement of Russia concerning Crimean independence "on the Declaration of independence of the Autonomous Republic of Crimea and Sevastopol to be a direct and undisguised interference of the Russian Federation in internal affairs of Ukraine, which is in odds with the fundamental principles of International Law and generally recognized principles of states coexistence."[76] The principles mentioned are found in the 1970 Declaration on Principles of International Law concerning Friendly Relations[77] which lays down that a state cannot interfere with the "territorial integrity or political unity of

---

[70] Dixon (n 67), 173.

[71] European Parliament, 'Position of Ukraine on the Russian Federation MFA's statement of 11 March on the Declaration of independence of the Autonomous Republic of Crimea and Sevastopil' (2014) < http://www.europarl.europa.eu/meetdocs/2009_2014/documents/d-ua/dv/dua_2014_0319_14_/dua_2014_0319_14_en.pdf> accessed 2 February 2015.

[72] Benjamin (n 47), 37.

[73] Vladislav Tolstykh, 'Reunification of Crimea with Russia: A Russian Perspective' [2014] C.J.I.L. 13(4), 881.

[74] *Ibid.*, 882.

[75] European Parliament (n 70).

[76] *Ibid.*

[77] United Nations General Assembly 'Declaration on Principles of International Law concerning Friendly Relations and Co-operation among States in accordance with the Charter of the United Nations' (24 October 1970) UN Doc A/RES/25/2625.

sovereign and independent states conducting themselves in compliance with the principle of equal rights and self-determination of peoples."[78]

Under the ICJ's *Advisory Opinion on Kosovo*[79] it was found that a declaration of independence did not violate international law but, in context, resulted from repeated denial of recognition by Serbia and a bloody conflict. The people of Crimea and Eastern Ukraine first needed to explore all avenues of political recourse as part of Ukraine and if Ukraine deny that opportunity the territories would in all likelihood be given international support to be independent. It must be noted that Russia does not recognise Kosovo as a state even though its declaration had been held to be legal. Crimea's referendum has been deemed illegal as the Crimean Parliament breached the Ukrainian Constitution and it is not clear the central government had not met the needs of Crimea. The Government of Ukraine pledged to hold elections, which took place in May, but many Eastern Ukrainians were not represented due to the conflict. Under those elections, the groups seeking self-determination would have been able to vote for candidates who supported independence or Russian integration. If, after the elections, the groups seeking self-determination were aggrieved by the results then a declaration of independence would not contravene international law and would be granted considerable weight if the international community could judge that those citizens were not sufficiently represented.

6. Conclusion

It is clear from the definitions in international law that Ukraine is a sovereign nation whose territorial integrity has been infringed by Russia. This has occurred due to the use of force in stationing Russian troops outside the agreed military bases in Crimea in contravention of the BSFA and the infringement of sovereignty by assisting rebels. Crimea was subjugated and whilst it declared itself a Russian federal state following a referendum, that referendum that has been deemed by the UN to be invalid. Russia as a permanent member paralysed the Security Council and the lack of a binding decision has led to the continued violation of Ukraine's sovereignty. The subjugation of Crimea and the status of rebels in East Ukraine would hold more credibility if all constitutional efforts had been explored in seeking self-determination and the interference of Russia cannot be justified. Russia can have no defence to its violation of Article 2(4) and the aforementioned regional treaties because no attack took place on its nationals, military or

[78] *Ibid.*, 7.

[79] *Accordance with International Law of the Unilateral Declaration of Independence in Respect of Kosovo* (Advisory Opinion) [2010] ICJ Rep 403.

territory; and former President Yanukovych was no longer in control of Ukraine when he asked for assistance and had been replaced by the democratic effort of appointing a new president by parliamentary vote.

On-going peaceful methods of resolution will hopefully bring an end to both the continued use of armed force and the gross violation of Ukraine's sovereignty. If civilian casualties persist a humanitarian crisis may result and the Security Council must attempt to re-establish international peace. Due to the aforementioned political constraints it is doubtful the Security Council would ever be able to pass a resolution under Articles 41 or 42 of the UN Charter for collective security measures. In the meantime, the international community must feel a "…sense of duty and responsibility to put pressure on Russia, in any way available, to show that it truly respects the principle of the rule of law, clearly and unambiguously."[80] Once Russian involvement ceases to be a factor, Ukraine will be free to decide its own destiny as a sovereign nation with the full support of the international community and the UN.

7. Bibliography

7.1. Cases

Accordance with International Law of the Unilateral Declaration of Independence in Respect of Kosovo (Advisory Opinion) [2010] ICJ Rep 403.

Legal Consequences of the Construction of a Wall in the Occupied Palestinian Territory (Advisory Opinion) [2004] ICJ Rep 136.

Military and Paramilitary Activities in and against Nicaragua (*Nicaragua v. United States of America*) [1986] ICJ Rep 14.

Oil Platforms (*Islamic Republic of Iran v. United States of America*) [2003] ICJ 4.

Re Kariņš and others v Parliament of Latvia and Cabinet of Ministers of Latvia [2007] Case No. 2007-10-0102 (Latvian Constitutional Court) (OUP Ref. ILDC 884 (LV 2007)).

Re Secession of Quebec [1998] 2 S.C.R. 217.

The Caroline [1837].

[80] Christopher Clement-Davies, 'Russia and the rule of law - again! The duty to speak out' [2014] I.E.L.R. 5, 155.

7.2. International Sources

Agreement between Ukraine and the Russian Federation on the Status and Conditions of Presence of the Black Sea Fleet of the Russian Federation in the Territory of Ukraine (adopted 28 May 1997).

Budapest Memorandum on Security Assurances (adopted 5 December 1994) UN Doc A/49/765.

Charter of the United Nations (adopted 24 October 1945).

Conference on Security and Co-operation in Europe Final Act (adopted 1 August 1975) (Organization for the Security and Co-operation in Europe).

International Covenant on Civil and Political Rights (adopted 16 December 1966, entered into force 23 March 1976) 999 UNTS 171 (ICCPR).

Treaty on Friendship, Cooperation, and Partnership between Ukraine and the Russian Federation (adopted 31 May 1997).

United Nations General Assembly 'Declaration on Principles of International Law concerning Friendly Relations and Co-operation among States in accordance with the Charter of the United Nations' (24 October 1970) UN Doc A/RES/25/2625.

UN General Assembly, 'Definition of Aggression' (14 December 1974) UN Doc A/RES/29/3314.

United Nations General Assembly 'Territorial Integrity of Ukraine' (1 April 2014) UN Doc A/RES/68/262.

UN Human Rights Council, 43rd Meeting (26th March 2009) Resolution 10/20

United Nations Security Council, Draft Resolution (15 March 2014) UN Doc S/2014/189.

United Nations Security Council, 2283rd Meeting (15 June 1981) UN Doc S/PV.2283.

United Nations Security Council, 7124th Meeting (1 March 2014) UN Doc S/PV.7124.

United Nations Security Council, 7134th Meeting (13 March 2014) UN Doc S/PV.7134.

United Nations Security Council, 7138th Meeting (15 March 2014) UN Doc S/PV.7138.

United Nations Security Council, 7157th Meeting (16 April 2014) UN Doc S/PV.7157.

United Nations Security Council, 7185th Meeting (28 May 2014) UN Doc S/PV.7185.

United Nations Security Council, 7219th Meeting (18 July 2014) UN Doc S/PV.7219.

United Nations Security Council, 7221st Meeting (21 July 2014) UN Doc S/PV.7221.

United Nations Security Council, 7287th Meeting (24 October 2014) UN Doc S/PV.7287.

7.3. Reports

International Commission on Intervention and State Sovereignty, 'The Responsibility To Protect' (Report of the ICISS, December 2001) < http://responsibilitytoprotect.org/ICISS%20Report.pdf> accessed 13 February 2015.

Norwegian Helsinki Committee, 'Ukraine, Russia crisis: breached of international law and human rights issues' (*NHC Policy Paper No.1 2014*, 20 March 2014) < http://www.nhc.no/filestore/Publikasjoner/Policy_Paper/NHC_PolicyPaper_1_2014UkraineQA.pdf> accessed 2 February 2015.

7.4. Books

Abass A, *International Law Text, Cases and Materials* (2nd edn, OUP, 2014).
Crawford J, *Brownlie's Principles of International Law* (8th edn, OUP, 2012).
Kaczorowska A, *Public International Law* (4th edn, Routledge, 2011).
Martin D, *International Law* (7th edn, OUP, 2013).

7.5. Journals

Allen S, 'What is Crimea's status in international law?' [2014] *S.L. Rev.* 73(Aut), 40-41.
Appleton S, 'Fighting for a better future' [2014] *IBA Global Insight*, Jun/Jul, 13-18.
Appleton S, Ivanova V, 'Ukraine: breaches of international law as crisis continues' [2014] *IBA Global Insight*, Apr/May.
Arend A, 'International Law and the Preemptive Use of Military Force' [2003] *The Washington Quarterly*, 26(2) 89–103.
Becker Lorca A, 'Petitioning the international: a "pre-history" of self-determination' [2014] *E.J.I.L.* 25(2), 497-523.
Benjamin T, 'Ukraine crisis' [2015] *IBA Global Insight*, Dec/Jan, 35-39.
Bilkova V, 'Belligerent reprisals in non-international armed conflicts' [2014] *I.C.L.Q.* 63(1), 31-65.
Clement-Davies C, 'Russia and the rule of law - again! The duty to speak out' [2014] *I.E.L.R.* 5, 155-156.
Conklin W, 'The peremptory norms of the international community' [2012] *E.J.I.L.* 23(3), 837-861.
Feldbrugge F, 'Ukraine, Russia and International Law' [2014] *Rev. C.E.E. Law* 39, 95-97.

Feldhusen A, 'Geography and the Boundaries of Confidence: The "Russian Factor" in Ukrainian Foreign Policy' [1999] 23 *Fletcher F. World Aff.* 119.

Herbach J, 'International and European Security Law' [2012] *Utrecht Journal of International and European Law*, 28(74), 1-3.

Khayre A, 'Self-defence, intervention by invitation, or proxy war? The legality of the 2006 Ethiopian invasion of Somalia' [2014] *A.J.I.C.L.* 22(2), 208-233.

Kretzmer D, 'The inherent right to self-defence and proportionality in jus ad bellum' [2013] *E.J.I.L.* 24(1), 235-282.

Lott A, 'The Tagliavini Report Revisited: Jus ad Bellum and the Legality of the Russian Intervention in Georgia' [2012] *Utrecht Journal of International and European Law*, 28(74), 4-21.

Mills A, 'The formalism of state sovereignty in territorial and maritime disputes' [2008] *C.L.J.* 67(3), 443-447.

Rees-Evans L, 'Secession and the use of force in international law' [2008] *C.S.L.R.* 4(2), 249-266.

Tolstykh V, 'Reunification of Crimea with Russia: A Russian Perspective' [2014] *C.J.I.L.* 13(4), 879-886.

7.6. Web Sources

'Debate Map: Ukraine Use of Force' (Oxford Public International Law, OUP, 3 August 2014) < http://opil.ouplaw.com/page/ukraine-use-of-force-debate-map#overview> accessed 2 February 2015.

'General Assembly Adopts Resolution Calling upon States Not to Recognize Changes in Status of Crimea Region' (United Nations Meetings Coverage & Press Releases, GA/11493, 27 March 2014) < http://www.un.org/press/en/2014/ga11493.doc.htm> accessed 2 February 2015.

'Nato accuses Russia of violating Ukraine sovereignty' (BBC News, 29 August 2014) <http://www.bbc.co.uk/news/world-europe-28984241> accessed 2 February 2015.

Adams P, 'Nato accuses Russia of violating Ukraine sovereignty' (BBC, 29 August 2014) < http://www.bbc.co.uk/news/world-europe-28984241> accessed 2 February 2015.

Council of the European Union, 'Council conclusions on Ukraine' (Press EN, Brussels, 15 August 2014) <http://www.europarl.europa.eu/meetdocs/2014_2019/documents/sede/dv/sede110914conclusionsukraine1508_/sede110914conclusionsukraine1508_en.pdf> accessed 11 February 2015.

Embassy of Ukraine to Japan, 'On Violations of Ukraine's Laws in Force and of Ukrainian-Russian Agreements by Military Units of the Black Sea Fleet of the Russian Federation in the Territory of Ukraine' (Ministry of Foreign Affairs of Ukraine, 3 March 2014) < http://mfa.gov.ua/en/news-feeds/foreign-offices-news/18622-shhodo-...sykih-ugod-vijsykovimi-formuvannyami-chf-rf-na-teritoriji-ukrajini> accessed 2 February 2015.

European Parliament, 'Position of Ukraine on the Russian Federation MFA's statement of 11 March on the Declaration of independence of the Autonomous Republic of Crimea and Sevastopil' (2014) < http://www.europarl.europa.eu/meetdocs/2009_2014/documents/d-ua/dv/dua_2014_0319_14_/dua_2014_0319_14_en.pdf> accessed 2 February 2015.

Hausler K, McCorquodale R, 'Ukraine Insta-Symposium: Crimea, Ukraine and Russia: Self-Determination, Intervention and International Law' (Opinio Juris, 10 March 2014) < http://opiniojuris.org/2014/03/10/ukraine-insta-symposium-crimea-ukraine-russia-self-determination-intervention-international-law/> accessed 2 February 2015.

Ignatzi C, 'Crimea: A breach of international law' (Deutsche Welle, 8 March 2014) < http://dw.de/p/1BMEj> accessed 2 February 2015.

Kimball S, 'Bound by treaty: Russia, Ukraine and Crimea' (Deutsche Welle, 11 March 2014) < http://www.dw.de/bound-by-treaty-russia-ukraine-and-crimea/a-17487632> accessed 2 February 2015.

Mandal R, 'Russia, Ukraine and International Law' (Chatham House, The Royal Institute of International Affairs, 7 March 2014) <https://www.chathamhouse.org/media/comment/view/198003#> accessed 2 February 2015.

McMahon R, 'Ukraine in Crisis' (Council on Foreign Relations, 25 August 2014) <http://www.cfr.org/ukraine/ukraine-crisis/p32540> accessed 2 February 2015.

Molloy A, 'Ukraine crisis: Russia is deliberately 'violating the independence and sovereignty of Ukraine', says William Hague' (The Independent, 14 April 2014) < http://www.independent.co.uk/news/world/europe/ukraine-crisis-russia-is-deliberately-violating-the-independence-and-sovereignty-of-ukraine-says-william-hague-9259024.html> accessed 2 February 2015.

Sari A, 'Ukraine Insta-Symposium: When does the Breach of a Status of Forces Agreement amount to an Act of Aggression? The Case of Ukraine and the Black Sea Fleet SOFA' (Opinio Juris, 6 March 2014) < http://opiniojuris.org/2014/03/06/ukraine-insta-symposium-breach-status-forces-agreement-amount-act-aggression-case-ukraine-black-sea-fleet-sofa/> accessed 2 February 2015.

Vaypan G, '(Un)Invited Guests: The Validity of Russia's Argument on Intervention by Invitation' (Cambridge Journal of International and

Comparative Law, 5 March 2014)<http://cjicl.org.uk/2014/03/05/uninvited-guests-validity-russias-argument-intervention-invitation/> accessed 3 February 2015.

Wisehart D, 'The Crisis in Ukraine and the Prohibition of the Use of Force: A Legal Basis for Russia's Intervention?' (Blog of the European Journal of International Law, 4 March 2014) <www.ejiltalk.org/the-crisis-in-ukraine-and-the-prohibition-of-the-use-of-force-a-legal-basis-for-russias-intervention/> accessed 3 February 2015.

Severing the Next Generation: Sexual Violence in Genocide[1]

Arsiné Grigoryan[2]

Genocide is the intent to destroy a particular group. Indeed, systematic mass murder is the most obvious way this intent materializes. Rape, while not readily apparent, is also an effective technique for perpetrators to execute genocide. During such a campaign, the targeted population is brutally tortured and murdered; however women, having a unique ability to carry the next generation, are strategically and perversely taken advantage of. The criminals responsible for such heinous acts are either not tried, or, even if they do stand trial, are held accountable for sexual violence, but not the genocide intent that motivates the rape. Sexual violence in the context of genocide is difficult to prosecute. While international laws have evolved over the years, they do not specifically identify how certain criminal acts fall under genocidal rape, making it problematic to determine liability. International courts and tribunals have struggled with defining rape as a tool of genocide. This article proposes a solution: an eight-factor balancing test that helps determine when a particular act of sexual violence crosses the line into genocide. The majority of these factors are drawn from international court cases as well as a famous psychological experiment.

Keywords: Genocide, International Law, Women's Rights, Human Rights, Crimes Against Humanity, Sexual Violence, Hague Conventions, Geneva Conventions, Rome Statute, Universal Declaration of Human Rights, Criminal Law.

---

[1] I dedicate this article in commemoration of the Armenian Genocide Centennial. I send my thanks to Professors D'Italia and Sloan for continuously challenging me, Judge Scott Gordon for his expertise, Professor Gowri Ramachandran for her guidance, and to my family and friends for their support.

[2] JD, Southwestern Law School; American Board of Trial Advocates Fellow; BA, Political Science and Media Studies, University of California, Berkeley.

1. INTRODUCTION

> Women were tortured. If a woman would not readily submit to sex with a gendarme, she was whipped, and if she tried to run away, she was shot. Once a young girl tried to run, the gendarme took out his sword and slashed her dress open, and she stood there with her young breasts naked, and he slashed each breast off her body, and they fell to the ground. I stared at the two small breasts lying on the ground. I stood frozen, then I just walked away. The girl bled to death next to her breasts. At night I lay on the ground and heard women screaming as they were raped. I listened to their voices echo in the immense dark desert air. There was no one, absolutely no one anywhere, to help us. Takooi, Hagop, Dikran and I slept on the ground together, almost as if we were attached to each other, as if we were one lump of a body. We hoped this would discourage the gendarmes from raping us, or from killing Hagop and Dikran.[3]

Genocide is undeniably one of the worst crimes. It degrades human beings, reduces them to worthless objects, and wipes them out through various acts that shock and terrorise a person. It is a meticulously planned out crime - systematic, clever, and merciless. Genocide is commonly understood as the killing of a particular group. It is not limited to murder with weapons, deliberate starvation, or the psychological cleansing of a group to force them to forget their identity. This question is, can it be rape?

Genocide has appeared all throughout the twentieth century. The Ottoman Empire primarily implemented desert marches.[4] The Nazis utilised gas chambers.[5] The Khmer Rouge used pick axes.[6] The Hutus made the machete notorious.[7] While the perpetrators had different weapons of choice, they all had one goal in common: destroy the targeted group.[8]

---

[3] Peter Balakian, *Black Dog of Fate* (Broadway Books, New York 1997) 219.

[4] Donald Bloxham, 'The Armenian Genocide of 1915-1916: Cumulative Radicalization and the Development of a Destruction Policy' (2003) 181 Past & Present 141, 180.

[5] Karen Remmler, 'Gender Identities and the Remembrance of the Holocaust' (1994) 10 Women in German Y.B. 167, 175.

[6] Loung Ung, *First They Killed My Father* (revd edn HarperCollins Publishers, New York 2000) 131.

[7] Philip Verwimp, 'Machetes and Firearms: The Organization of Massacres in Rwanda' (2006) 43 *J. Peace & Res.* 5, 5.

[8] In "total war," sexual violence during genocide is not only used to destroy the existence of a particular group, but it can also be a technique to demoralise that group and take away their will to fight. Statement by Caroline C. Morales, Lieutenant Colonel, US Army, (Personal email correspondence 2 December 2014).

In the course of the destruction of the group, many of the genocides included the rape of both men and women.[9] There is absolutely no justification for rape or sexual assault, including a military excuse.[10] As explored later in this paper, the rapes were different in each genocide. Nevertheless, any sexual violence committed to further genocide, despite its varying nature, still needs to be recognised and prosecuted as a tactic of the genocide.

Rafael Lemkin[11] coined the term "genocide."[12] The Convention on the Prevention and Punishment of the Crime of Genocide [hereinafter the Genocide Convention] was adopted on December 9, 1948, with Article II defining genocide:

> ...with the intent to destroy, in whole or in part, a national, ethnical, racial or religious group, such as (a) Killing members of the group; (b) Causing serious bodily or mental harm to members of the group; (c) Deliberately inflicting on the group conditions of life calculated to bring about its physical destruction in whole or in part; (d) Imposing measures intended to prevent births within the group; (e) Forcibly transferring children of the group to another group."[13]

While Article I states that genocide is still genocide whether it is committed during war or peace, much of genocide has occurred in the time of war.[14]

From a legal standpoint, genocide is a complex crime because it involves multiple parties and fading memories from witness testimony. As such, the resulting court judgments rely upon hundreds of pages of witness testimony,

---

[9] Throughout this article, I use the word "woman" but am not necessarily referring to a female over the age of eighteen years. To say that I am referring to a woman of childbearing age would also be inadequate since a young girl could get raped without yet entering adolescence. While she cannot bear a child at that stage in her life, she may be traumatised and not have sexual intercourse for a long time, and thus not have children of her own to further the race she identifies with. In other words "woman" in this paper broadly refers to any female.

[10] M C Bassiouni, *Crimes Against Humanity in International Criminal Law* (2nd edn Kluwer Law International, The Hague 1999) 344.

[11] Lemkin, a Polish Jew, was a lawyer who played a primary role in defining genocide. While still a young student studying law in Europe, following the acquittal of Solomon Tehlirian who was accused for murdering Talaat Pasha, Lemkin hotly debated with his professor, arguing that instead the perpetrators should have been on trial. Philippe Sands, 'A Memory of Justice: The Unexpected Place of Lviv in International Law – A Personal History' (2011) 43 *Case W. Res. Int'l L.* 739, 784.

[12] Benjamin B. Ferencz, 'International Trials for Internal Armed Conflicts' (2001) 95 *Am. J. Int'l L.* 35.

[13] Convention on the Prevention and Punishment of the Crime of Genocide, opened for signature Dec. 9, 1948, 102 Stat. 3045, 78 UNTS 277

[14] *Ibid.*

and numerous perpetrators and victims to help establish and decide a case. This paper focuses primarily on characterising rapes in such a manner that will make it easier for judges in international courts and tribunals to differentiate between rapes that happen to occur during genocide and rapes that occur in furtherance of genocide. Since the objective here is to punish perpetrators, the lenses of prosecutors will help achieve the goal. However, the viewpoint of other parties - the accused, the witness, the victim and the judge—becomes helpful when writing a statute that will be just.

The very definition of genocide means that the perpetrators will not show mercy on any group of the targeted population. Indeed, Dr. Nazim Mehemed, a criminal figure during the Armenian Genocide remarked that it is "essential that no Armenian survives."[15] In the systematic killings, the intelligentsia were often killed first, for the reason of destroying cultural, religious, and political leaders in the group that have influence on the success and advancement of the population.[16] Next in line were the men. Last on the list were typically the elderly, women, and children. The women—able to carry the next generation—had a unique ability that would be taken advantage of.

Thus, to better serve the fundamental rights and interests of women, as well as prosecute genocide more comprehensively, international courts should utilise an eight-factor balancing test to determine whether rape is used as a tool of genocide and punish accordingly. First, this paper will examine how international laws have evolved to deal with genocide. Next, it will establish how rape is a potent tool in genocide, either through forced impregnation or otherwise. Here, specific incidents will illustrate this phenomenon, drawing from international cases. Third and finally, to clear up any complexities international judges face in determining whether rape can be a tool of genocide, this paper proposes an eight-factor balancing test.

2. Current International Law on Genocide and Rape

The international world is anarchic.[17] There is no one governing body of law that helps piece statutes together; nor does one single court handle every international conflict proceeding.[18] Various international laws acknowledge

[15] Paul R. Bartrop and Samuel Totten, *Dictionary of Genocide* (Greenwood, Westport 2007) 303

[16] Norman Davies, 'Foreward' in *Richard C. Lukas, Forgotten Holocaust: The Poles Under German Occupation, 1939-1994* 8 (Hippocrene Books rev. ed. 2001). Richard C. Lukas, *Forgotten Holocaust: The Poles Under German Occupation, 1939-1944* (revd edn Hippocrene Books, USA 2001) 8.

[17] Lecture by Ronald Hassner, Professor, University of California, Berkeley entitled 'War!' (12 November 2009).

[18] *Ibid.*

atrocities, but do not always specifically identify which criminal acts are considered atrocities, rendering it difficult to determine liability. A balancing test, clarifying the definition of genocidal rape, would remedy that problem. While international law does not explicitly address genocidal rape, the application of these laws, in effect, outlaw genocidal rape.

The Hague Conventions of 1899 and 1907 were some of the earlier statutes to set the stage for human rights law. Rape was merely implied as a violation, masked under the wording of "family honour and rights" in Article 46 of the 1907 Hague Convention. It did not "explicitly condemn rape."[19] This vague and discriminatory phrasing reflected the marginal role of women in society at the time. Still, the Hague Conventions were the mother of the treaties and laws that came after. Many of the ideas in the Hague Conventions were later codified in the Geneva Conventions.[20] The inception of most of these laws occurred at the end of World War II. One such document that emerged was the Universal Declaration of Human Rights.[21]

Even in its preamble, the Universal Declaration of Human Rights [hereinafter UDHR] notes that ignoring basic human rights only leads to "barbarous acts which have outraged the conscience of mankind."[22] In fact, all acts committed in the course of genocide, including the horrific acts of rape, are barbarous in nature. Article 4 forbids slavery in all its possible forms.[23] Many genocide victims were forced into labour.[24] These forms of slavery often included different types of torture, including beatings and rapes.[25] Article 5 condemns torture, or any kind of "cruel, inhuman or degrading treatment…" towards anyone.[26] Torture is explicitly forbidden and prohibitions against genocide are certainly implicit.[27]

The UDHR also values and protects the family and motherhood. Article 16(3) recognises that "family is the national and fundamental group unit of society and is entitled to protection by society and the State."[28] During genocide, families are often separated - men are typically tortured and killed

---

[19] Matthew Lippman, 'Humanitarian Law: War on Women' (2000) 9 *MSU-DCL J. Int'l L.* 33, 37.

[20] Bassiouni, *supra* n 8, 331.

[21] Universal Declaration of Human Rights (adopted 10 December 1948 UNGA Res 217 A(III) (UDHR)

[22] *Id.*

[23] *Id.*

[24] Ung, *supra* note at 4, 56-57.

[25] *International Court of Justice (ICJ): Bosnia and Herzegovina v. Serbia and Montenegro*, 46 Int'l Legal Materials, 188, 254 (2007).

[26] Universal Declaration of Human Rights, *supra* note at 18.

[27] Hurst Hannum, 'The Status of the Universal Declaration of Human Rights in National and International Law' (1995/1996) 25 *Ga. J. Int'l & Comp. L.* 287, 342

[28] Universal Declaration of Human Rights, *supra* note at 18.

and women are raped.[29] The intentional splitting of families stirs and harms a targeted population. Children are the future of the population the family identifies itself with. Killing, inflicting bodily harm, and creating such conditions that will destroy the group are tactics that fall directly within the definition of genocide. Article 25(2) of the UDHR declares that "Motherhood and childhood are entitled to special care and assistance. All children, whether born in or out of wedlock, shall enjoy the same social protection." This concept, given special attention in this famous document, emphasises the importance of mothers in a society. Thus, the destruction of women through rape, who either have children or may have children of their own ethnic group in the future, advances the goal of genocide. Rape during genocide undoubtedly violates several human rights guarantees of the UDHR.

Geneva Convention (III) relative to the Treatment of Prisoners of War of 12 August 1949[30] [hereinafter the Third Geneva Convention] highlights the required humane treatment during times of war. Article 3 focuses on "armed conflict not of an international character" and protects civilians, "including those placed 'hors de combat'" condemning "cruel treatment and torture" and "outrages upon personal dignity, in particular humiliating and degrading treatment."[31] The targeted population of genocide suffers various atrocities, not limited to rape, intended to humiliate and degrade individuals. Perpetrators would even molest children.[32] Article 14 guarantees that "Women shall be treated with all the regard due to their sex and shall in all cases benefit by treatment as favourable as that granted to men."[33] This is meant to be understood as women not being raped, forced in prostitution, and attacked sexually in any way. The direct reference "to their sex" specifies crimes historically unique to that of women. Article 130 introduces the idea of "Grave breaches" being "wilful killing, torture or inhuman treatment . . . , wilfully causing great suffering or serious injury to body or health, . . ." which is one of the provisions many genocide perpetrators are charged under.

The most relevant articles in the Geneva Convention (IV) relative to the Protection of Civilian Persons in Time of War of 12 August 1949[34] [hereinafter the Fourth Geneva Convention] are Articles 27 and 147. Article

---

[29] During the Bosnian Genocide, Edina's family was separated several times while they were fleeing from place to place. At some point, when her father discovered his brother was blown up by a bomb, he and his son went to retrieve his various body parts to give him a proper funeral with the family. Telephone interview with Edina Fifić, Bosnian Genocide survivor conducted by the author on 24 September 2013.

[30] Geneva Convention Relative to the Treatment of Prisoners of War, August 12, 1949, 6 U.S.T. 3316, 75 U.N.T.S. 135.

[31] *Id.*

[32] Rosemary H. Cohen, *The Survivor* (Lico Publishing 2002) 158.

[33] *Id.*

[34] Geneva Convention Relative to the Protection of Civilian Persons in Time of War, August 12, 1949, 6 U.S.T. 3316, 75 UNTS 135.

27 provides that, "Women shall be especially protected against any attack on their honour, in particular against rape, enforced prostitution, or any form of indecent assault."[35] During genocide, acts of rape are not only abundant, but also a powerful tool in the execution of the genocide. In Article 147, the phrase "unlawful deportation or transfer or unlawful confinement of a protected person" is added to the "Grave breaches."[36] In many genocides, the perpetrators deported the targeted population to camps. In the Armenian Genocide, Armenian women and children were forced out of their land into desert marches where they would die of starvation.[37]

The Protocol Additional to the Geneva Conventions of 12 August 1949, and relating to the Protection of Victim's of International Armed Conflicts (Protocol I), 8 June 1977[38] [hereinafter Protocol I] provide two significant Articles. First, Article 75(2)(b) condemns "outrages upon personal dignity, in particular humiliating and degrading treatment, enforced prostitution and any form of indecent assault."[39] Such treatment during genocide included public rapes, abduction, and mutiliation of sexual organs. Second, Article 76 entitled "Protection of Women" demands that "Women . . . be the object of special respect and . . . protected in particular against rape, forced prostitution and any other form of indecent assault."[40] Again, both these provisions aim to protect women in times of war and internal conflict. Protocol Additional to the Geneva Conventions of 12 August 1949, and relating to the Protection of Victims of Non-International Armed Conflicts (Protocol II), 8 June 1977[41] [hereinafter Protocol II] expands on some protections. Article 4 promises protection from terrorism, rape, slavery, and mutilation to name a few. Mutilation typically went hand-in-hand with rape in that women's reproductive organs were also mutilated with weapons after a rape or series of rapes. An exception to such mutilation would be when the genocide perpetrators intended to impregnate the women and thus needed their reproductive organs to be healthy when delivering the baby.

After the tragedies of World War II, the Agreement for the Prosecution and Punishment of the Major War Criminals of the European axis, and Charter of the International Military Tribunal [hereinafter the London Charter]

---

[35] *Id.*
[36] *Id.*
[37] Balakian, *supra* note 1, at 52-53.
[38] Protocol Additional to the Geneva Conventions of August 12, 1949, and relating to the Protection of Victims of International Armed Conflicts (Protocol I), June 8, 1977, 1125 UNTS 3.
[39] *Id.*
[40] *Id.*
[41] Protocol Additional to the Geneva Conventions of August 12, 1949, and relating to the Protection of Victims of Non-International Armed Conflicts (Protocol II), June 8, 1977, 1125 UNTS 609.

was created August 8, 1945 in essence to punish the criminal activity of the Nazis.[42] The Nuremberg trials, while they addressed many crimes, did not include rape.[43] Commonly known as the Tokyo Charter - the London Charter's counterpart of the "Far East" - also does not mention rape.[44]

The Nuremberg Trials, the first genocide prosecutions, paved the road for future genocide perpetrators to be brought to justice. Twelve landmark cases following World War II helped punish individuals who carried out the genocidal goals of Adolf Hitler and his Nazi regime. One of those cases was *U.S. v. Ohlendorf. et al.*,[45] also known as the "Einsatzgruppen Case." The defendants were twenty-three Nazis holding various positions charged with the "systematic program of genocide" under Count I - Crimes Against Humanity.[46]

While there was no discussion about sexual violence, some reference was made about banning sexual relations with another group. It was clear that the Nazi agenda aimed to purify the German race with various laws in place. Paragraph 2(d) of the judgment mentioned the "Executing, imprisoning in concentration camps, or Germanizing Eastern workers and prisoners of war who had had sexual intercourse With Germans, and imprisoning the Germans involved."[47] Further, paragraph 14 showed the "Punishment for Sexual Intercourse with Germans. Czechs, Poles and other Eastern workers or prisoners of war who had had sexual intercourse with Germans were examined by the racial examiners of RuSHA. Those who were found to be not "racially desirable" were imprisoned in concentration camps or executed. Those found "racially valuable" were Germanized."[48] Interracial sexual intercourse was seen as tainting the German race. To prevent that, this rule was in place by the Nazi regime to keep the German race pure. In fact, under the Nazi Regime, German women were seen as "breeding machines."[49] Years later, when the Bosnian Genocide occurred, Serbian forces used similar tactics. When the Serbs raped the Bosnians and detained them until they gave birth, they essentially cleansed the newborns into becoming Serbs.[50] The difference between what happened in the Holocaust and what happened in the

---

[42] Henry Morgenthau, Jr., former U.S. Secretary of Treasury and son of Henry Morgenthau, Sr., was also present. Henry T. King, Jr., 'The Legacy of Nuremberg' (2002) 34 *Case W. Res. Int'l L.* 335, 336

[43] Bassiouni, *supra* note 8, at 344.

[44] *Id.*

[45] IV Trials Of War Criminals Before The Nuremberg Military Tribunals Under Control Council Law No. 10 411 (1947-1948).

[46] *Id.* at 166 **para.** 3.

[47] *Id.* at 166.

[48] *Id.* at 170.

[49] Lippman, *supra* note 16, at 48.

[50] Emma Lindsay, 'Lysistrata, Women, & War: International Law's Treatment of Women in Conflict and Post-Conflict Situations' (2005) 12 *Tex. Wesleyan L. Rev.* 345, 352

Bosnian Genocide was that the Serbs set out to rape Bosnian women as part of their genocide campaign, whereas the Germans forbade even consensual intercourse with another ethnicity. Rassenschande, racial defilement, was a crime in Nazi Germany.[51] If such sexual relations did occur, then the other ethnicity would be "Germanized."

The Rome Statute of the International Criminal Court[52] [hereinafter Rome Statute] divides international crimes in four sections: genocide, crimes against humanity, war crimes, and the crime of aggression. For purposes of this paper, the first three are relevant. Article 6 utilises the definition of the Genocide Convention when explaining what genocide means.[53] Article 7 deals with the crimes against humanity indicating that "knowledge of the attack" as a "widespread or systematic attack directed" is necessary.[54] This element is one of the determinative factors that can aid judges in deciding when rape crosses the fine line and becomes a tool of genocide. Enslavement, torture, and rape are listed among other crimes. Subsection (g) provides "Rape, sexual slavery, enforced prostitution, forced pregnancy, enforced sterilization, or any other form of sexual violence of comparable gravity."[55] It encompasses a range of sexually violent acts. Therefore, vaginal penetration is not the only way perpetrators can be punished for rape as genocide. Section 2(c) of Article 7 describes "Enslavement" to be the "attaching to the right of ownership over a person and includes the exercise of such power in the course of trafficking in persons, in particular women and children."[56] Many women were sold as sex slaves during a genocide. Subsection (e) defines torture as "the intentional infliction of severe pain or suffering, whether physical or mental, upon a person in the custody or under the control of the accused…"[57] The victims of rape, if not dead, suffer a great deal of physical as well as mental pain. Subsection (f) describes "Forced pregnancy" as the "unlawful confinement of a woman forcibly made pregnant, with the intent of affecting the ethnic composition of any population…"[58] One of the main tactics utilised in the Bosnian Genocide was forced pregnancy as a means to wipe out the Bosnian group. Article 8 entitled "War crimes" borrows the "Grave breaches" provision of the Geneva Conventions.[59] The Rome Statute also indicates that

---

[51] Robert Gellately, 'The Gestapo and German Society: Political Denunciation in the Gestapo Case Files' (1988) 60 *The J. of Modern History* 654, 671

[52] Rome Statute of the International Criminal Court, U.N. Doc A/CONF. 183/9 (1998) 2187 UNTS 90.

[53] *Id.*

[54] *Id.*

[55] *Id.*

[56] *Id.*

[57] *Id.*

[58] Rome Statute, *supra* note 48.

[59] *Id.*

sexual violence as defined in Article 7, amounts to a grave breach as well under the Geneva Conventions.[60] Among numerous other crimes, the perpetrators of the Bosnian and Rwandan Genocides were charged with "grave breaches."

The above are the main authorities when it comes to international human rights law. Plenty of provisions in each of these statutes have been violated in the course of genocide, particularly through the acts of rape. However, these statutes fall short of helping international courts and tribunals determine when and how rape becomes a tool of genocide. At most, they outlaw the crime, but fail to guide the courts in assessing how the rape is a tool of the genocide. A balancing test will help bridge this gap.

3. Rape as a Tool of Genocide

In the context of genocide, the perpetrator rapes as one of the ways to assert his power over the victims of the targeted group. This assertion of dominance over the weaker group furthers the goal of genocide as it is fatal, even prompting victims to commit suicide.[61] Eyewitness accounts of the Armenian Genocide describe hundreds of women holding hands and leaping into the waters of the Euphrates River to escape the fate of being raped as hysteria swept over them.[62] The motives for such a choice included constantly observing violence, rape, and abduction, losing family members, and "abandon[ing] hope of survival."[63] The act of power performed directly on the human body destroys it.[64] Since genocide is the wiping out of a group, rape achieves this by collectively harming the bodies of the group--either directly by raping them, or indirectly by forcing them to take their own lives.

Women and men have different biological makeups. While both have the power to reproduce offspring, women carry the children inside their wombs. The form and function of a woman's body makes some crimes easier for the terrorising group. In some ways, that ability to bear children becomes a curse to the woman when she is sexually violated in genocide. Regardless of how the perpetrator executed the rape, the woman still suffers in some form or another. For instance, foreign-object penetration—the insertion of an object into the "vaginal, rectal, oral, or other orifice" of a person—can be just as

---

[60] *Id.*

[61] Donald E. Miller and Lorna Touryan Miller, *Survivors: An Oral History of the Armenian Genocide* (University of California Press, Berkeley 1999) 103-104.

[62] *Ibid.*

[63] *Ibid.*

[64] Writer and director Pier P. Pasolini, before being assassinated after the conclusion of his horrific film, expressed such views as the basis for the notorious film in the DVD extra features. *Salo* (Produzioni Europee Associati 1975).

emotionally and physically hurtful as vaginal-penal penetration.[65] It can even be fatal, as illustrated in the "game of swords," where Turkish gendarmes during the Armenian Genocide forced women to sit naked on swords in the ground so that it would slice through the women's vaginas, impaling them.[66] This mutilated the very organ responsible for childbearing, and killed the woman with the act of foreign-object penetration. During the Second Sino-Japanese War, Chinese women from all social classes were raped numerous times, and some even gang-raped to death.[67] Mutilation was not uncommon. In one account, Japanese soldiers 'rammed a stick' inside of an elderly woman.[68] During the Armenian Genocide, if women survived rape, many were traumatised for a long time and would not allow other men to touch them.[69] This in turn would prevent them from giving birth and having children within their race. Pregnant women evoked absolutely no mercy from the Turkish gendarmes. In many instances, the bellies of women were slashed, killing both the women of the group and their children who would be the next generation of that group.[70] Similar incidents occurred in Nanking during the Second-Sino Japanese War.[71] During the Liberation War of Bangladesh, Dr. Geoffrey Davis, who treated rape victims, learned that General Tikka Khan gave orders to rape and impregnate roughly 200,000–400,000 Bengali women so that the "whole generation of children in East Pakistan" would be "born with the blood of the West."[72] These atrocities reappeared in the Bosnian Genocide, where women were raped and forced to bear the children of the hostile party, as the nightmare would continue for another nine months or more.[73] Serbian soldiers would often use the term "planting their seed" when raping the Bosnian Muslim women.[74] These rapes were not for the sole purpose of satisfying the perpetrators' sexual needs. These rapes were

---

[65] Merril D. Smith, *Encyclopedia of Rape* (Greenwood, Westport 2004) 79.

[66] *Ravished Armenia* (First National Pictures 1919). Considered a "lost work" a portion of the film was recently recovered. The film documents all the tragedies that teenager Aurora Mardiganian witnessed and experienced. She actually stars in the film. Henry Morgenthau, Sr., ambassador to Turkey during the Armenian Genocide, was also in the film. *Auction of Souls*, IMDb, <http://www.imdb.com/title/tt0009892/> (last visited 13 January 2015).

[67] Iris Chang, *The Rape of Nanking: The Forgotten Holocaust of World War II* (Penguin Books, New York 1997) 90

[68] *Id.* at 91.

[69] Aurora Mardiganian was one of the many women traumatised at the touch of a man after her experiences in the Armenian Genocide. Anthony Slide, Writer and Film Expert, Glendale Public Library: Ravished Armenia Lecture (24 March 2013).

[70] Cohen, *supra* note 30, at 59.

[71] Chang, *supra* note 65, at 91.

[72] Bina D'Costa, '1971: Rape and its consequences' *Bangladesh News 24* (Bangladesh 15 December 2010) <http://opinion.bdnews24.com/2010/12/15/1971-rape-and-its-consequences> accessed 10 May 2015.

[73] Telephone interview with Edina Fifić, *supra* note 26.

[74] *Id.*

implemented as a tool of genocide - an intentional tactic to destroy Bosnian ethnicity and society.[75] It was meant to embarrass, degrade, and terrify a targeted group.[76] Indeed, public rapes were intended to terrorise a particular population and force them into fleeing.[77] More recently, in the Rwandan Genocide, "women and younger men were especially targeted" because they "represented the future of the Tutsi minority."[78] Women were raped and often killed, a "pattern reminiscent of the Armenian Genocide."[79] Perpetrators throughout history recycled genocide tactics, including systematic rape.

Some of the notorious perpetrators of the Bosnian Genocide were tried in the Netherlands. In *Prosecutor v. Kunarac*,[80] three defendants, Dragoljib Kunarac, Radomir Kovac, and Zoran Vukovic were charged with crimes relating to sexual violence, including torture, rape, enslavement, and outrages upon personal dignity. All of these were crimes against humanity.[81] Charges were brought under the ICTY statute and the Geneva Conventions.[82] Many of the rapes occurred in or near Foca High School, where many women were detained.[83] Among several rape victims was Witness FSW-87, who testified she felt she was "owned" by Kovac as she was forced to "undress" and dance naked on a table.[84] Witness FSW-75 remembers that she was raped "while the Swan Lake was playing" in the background.[85] Finally, witness FWS-191 admitted she was a virgin before getting raped.[86] Kunarac replied that he would be her first.[87] Kunarac was armed with a weapon and out of intense fear, the young victim was so "rigid" that he could not penetrate her vagina.[88]

The victims who took the witness stand to tell their stories were all Bosnian women who were raped because they were part of the targeted group. Their identity was the primary reason they were raped. Thus, in its analysis of

---

[75] Beth Stephens, 'Humanitarian Law and Gender Violence: An End to Centuries of Neglect?' (1999) 3 *Hofstra L. & Pol'Y Symp*. 87, 90

[76] *Id*. at 91.

[77] *Id*.

[78] Kristen Renwick Monroe, *Ethics in an Age of Terror and Genocide: Identity and Moral Choice* (Princeton University Press, Princeton 2011) 356-357

[79] *Id*.

[80] Case No. IT-96-23-T & IT-96-23/1-T, Judgment (Int'l Crim. Trib. for the Former Yugoslavia Feb. 22, 2001).

[81] While most of the crimes the perpetrators were charged with were direct violations of the Geneva Conventions as well as other international laws, each tribunal had its own charging statute created for the trials to help draw parameters to prosecute the accused. Interview with Scott Gordon, Judge at Stanley Mosk Courthouse (Los Angeles 18 October 2013).

[82] *Kunarac* **para.** 7-8.

[83] *Id*. **para.** 32.

[84] *Id*. **para.** 71.

[85] *Id*. **para.** 178.

[86] *Id*. **para.** 259.

[87] *Kunarac* **para.** 259.

[88] *Id*.

the case, the Tribunal indicated that "as long as there is a link with the widespread or systematic attack against a civilian population, a single act could qualify as a crime against humanity."[89] In other words, the perpetrators need to possess knowledge that the rapes they committed were acts to foster the genocide. The actual number of criminal acts is not of huge significance.[90] The Tribunal also noted the "organized nature" and "patterns" of the rapes.[91] This showed that the mass rapes were not random or meaningless; rather, they were systemised to destroy and terrorise the Bosnian population.

The Bosnian Genocide rapes were meant to "achieve military objectives."[92] These rapes were committed in masses. For both Muslims and Serbs, the male's identity determines the ethnicity of the child.[93] This helps explain why such a policy was in place for Serbian men to rape Bosnian women. It would break the link between the mother and the child. Also, it would sever the next generation of Bosnian identity.

In genocide, a perpetrator need not physically rape a single woman in order to be guilty of the crime. The prosecutions in the ICTR have helped expand the meaning of genocide to include rape.[94] Jean-Paul Akayesu was a central figure in the Rwanda Genocide. The evidence presented in the court showed that he did not get his hands dirty by killing anyone.[95] He also did not rape anyone. However, he was eventually charged with genocide.[96] Not only was he charged with counts of rape, but the Tribunal acknowledged that he, "by his own words, specifically ordered, instigated, aided and abetted . . . acts of sexual violence."[97] The fact that Akayesu did not rape women himself, but urged and let it happen, illuminates an important point: an official's orders to rape the Tutsi women provided clear evidence of a plan of genocide. Evidence strongly shows that women were raped because of the mere fact that they were of the Tutsi ethnic group. Indeed, the court emphasised that the rapes were "systematic" and "perpetrated against all Tutsi women and solely against them."[98] Moreover, a Tutsi woman that was "married to a Hutu" claims that "she was not raped because her ethnic background was unknown."[99]

---

[89] *Id.* **para.** 417.
[90] *Id.*
[91] *Id.* **para.** 259.
[92] Siobahn K. Fisher, 'Occupation of the Womb: Forced Impregnation as Genocide' (1996) 46 *Duke L.J.* 91, 91-128.
[93] *Id.* at 114.
[94] Alexandra A. Miller, 'From the International Criminal Tribunal for Rwanda to the International Criminal Court: Expanding the Definition of Genocide to Include Rape' (2003) 108 Penn. St. L. Rev. 349, 350.
[95] *Prosecutor v. Akayesu* (Judgment) Case No. ICTR-96-4-T (2 September 1998).
[96] *Akayesu* **para.** 734.
[97] *Id.* **para.** 692.
[98] *Id.* **para.** 732.
[99] *Id.*

This direct testimony further solidifies the concept that rapes were used as a powerful weapon in genocide against women of the target group. Article II(b) of the Genocide Convention included "serious bodily or mental harm" to the individuals of a particular population as a campaign of genocide.[100] The ICTR recognised rape as an extremely effective way to cause serious bodily injury and mental harm on the Tutsi women, thereby accelerating the annihilation of the Tutsi population.[101]

A "mob psychology" that seems to be always present in genocide, "create[s] an atmosphere favourable to the perpetration of the crime" by placing blame for various "difficulties" on the other party.[102] The judgment in *Akayesu* examined this psychological manipulation to establish that incitement to commit genocide can be both direct and implicit.[103] It is not surprising that such a tactic appeared in all genocides, notably in the first genocide of the twentieth century, where step three of the systematic genocide planned to "Excite Moslem opinion" with ill-emotions against their Christian Armenian population.[104] Evidence suggests that the thoughts of the perpetrating party must be tainted with hatred so that they can carry out various crimes, including the mass rape of women.

Women are able to carry in their bodies the next generation of their ethnic group. These horrid acts of sexual violence sever ties with the previous generation. Systematic rapes during genocide aim to destroy a society since women play a crucial role in the continuity of their culture and ethnicity.[105] Hence, damaging women's ability to help in the physical and cultural advancement of that society, shatters the group, thereby furthering the objective of genocide.[106] Rape is therefore a tool of genocide.

4. Proposed Test for International Courts and Tribunals

Much of the terminology in the international law and charging statutes intermix. Sexual violence is "torture" and "inhuman treatment" as indicated in the Geneva Conventions. However, torture and inhuman treatment do not always include rape. Torture can include whipping, waterboarding, and

---

[100] Genocide Convention, *supra* note 10.

[101] Sherrie L. Russell-Brown, 'Rape as an Act of Genocide' *(2003)* 21 *Berkeley J. Int'l L.* 350, 352.

[102] *Akayesu* **para.** 557.

[103] José E. Alvarez, 'Lessons From the Akayesu Judgment' (1999) 5 *ILSA J. Int'l & Comp. L.* 359, 361.

[104] Manus I. Midlarsky, *The Killing Trap: Genocide in the Twentieth Century* (Cambridge University Press, New York 2005) 159-160.

[105] Stephens, *supra* note 67, at 89.

[106] *Id.*

beating just to name a few. The term "inhuman treatment" encompasses a wide range of acts. Yet, rape is a distinct act that can have consequences which include pregnancy, childbirth, abortion, damage to the vagina and other parts, "occupation" of the womb preventing the woman from having a child with a man of her own group since she is presently carrying the child of perpetrator, and a sign of shame in various societies even today.[107] Thus, rape victims tend to suffer from severe psychological damage such as feelings of lowered self-worth.[108] This can result in the victims not being able to have normal sexual or childbearing experiences with individuals of their own choosing.[109] As such, the very act of rape, especially a series of rapes as a means of destroying a group, clearly amounts to genocide. Genocide is a term not to be applied loosely and inserting the terms "sexual violence" somewhere in the definition will open it up to all kinds sexual violence that are not genocide. To prevent this from occurring, a balancing test is necessary to allow tribunal judges to weigh the evidence and make a fair decision.

4.1. Current ICC Statute

The current ICC Statute, while it does not include such a balancing test, does establish elements of rape. The ICC Statute explicitly mentions the invasion of the human body with a "sexual organ or of the anal or genital opening of the victim with any object or any other part of the body."[110] The inclusion of foreign-object penetration is helpful in the context of genocide in that it establishes that the physical and psychological effect of the rape can still be the same. Foreign-object penetration "further humiliates the victim" since it sexually violates the human body with an inanimate object "while amplifying the power of the attacker."[111] Even if the perpetrators are not raping with their own bodies, the rapes can nonetheless kill the woman and destroy the group. The second part of the statute focuses on "force" as well as a "coercive environment" where victims can be easily taken advantage of.[112] For instance, in the Bosnian Genocide, women were held in various camps and brought out to be raped.[113]

---

[107] Fisher, *supra* note 82, at 92.
[108] *Id.*
[109] *Id.*
[110] M C Bassiouni, *Introduction to International Criminal Law* (2nd revd edn Martinus Nijhoff Publishers, Leiden 2013) 192-93.
[111] Smith, *supra* note 63, at 79.
[112] Bassiouni, *supra* note 108, at 192-93.
[113] William B. Wood 'Geographic Aspects of Genocide: A Comparison of Bosnia and Rwanda' (2001) 26 Transactions of the Institute of British Geographers 57, 68

These elements are broad enough that they include various aspects of rape, but not too broad so that they are vague or confusing. In addition to these elements, a judge can apply the following factors to determine whether rape has been committed as part of genocide.

4.2. The Balancing Test: Eight Factors

Judges in international courts and tribunals should weigh the following factors: (1) Orders from a high ranking authority; (2) Creating a hostile environment that allows for sexual violence to occur; (3) Presence of military personnel; (4) Rape performed as a "spectacle"[114]; (5) Pattern of behavior; (6) Uniform dress; (7) Derogatory words used during the sexual violence; and (8) Forced impregnation as a result of the rape or intent and knowledge to kill as a result of the sexual violence.

4.2.1. Orders from a high ranking authority

The first factor directly shows that the authoritative figures pushed for sexual violence. These high-ranking individuals are most likely also in charge of the outlining the plan of genocide. "Do to them whatever you wish," is one example of an actual military command authorising the "full right of usage" of women.[115] In the *Kunarac* judgment, a witness testified that soldiers were ordered to rape women.[116] A famous study by Stanley Milgram[117] proved that people follow the orders of a person in authority, no matter how inhumane the orders are.[118] Thus, immediate orders from an authoritative figure are a strong indicator that the rape was part of a genocide campaign to eliminate a group.

4.2.2. Hostile environment

The second factor is just a more subtle way of encouraging the sexual violence. The "mob psychology" language in *Akayesu* inspires this factor.

---

[114] Catherine A. MacKinnon 'Rape, Genocide, and Women's Human Rights' (1994) 17 Harv. Women's L. J. 5, 12.

[115] Taner Akçam, *The Young Turks' Crime Against Humanity: The Armenian Genocide and Ethnic Cleansing in the Ottoman Empire* (Human Rights and Crimes Against Humanity, Princeton University Press, Princeton 2013) 312.

[116] *Kunarac* para. 39.

[117] Stanley Milgram, *Obedience to Authority: An Experimental View* (Perennial Classics, New York 2009) 1 Milgram's motivation for this experiment came from the fact that his parents were Holocaust survivors.

[118] *Id.* at 12-13.

Even where implicit or public incitement is unsuccessful, *Akayesu* made it clear that the attempt is punishable.[119] Similarly, even if individuals failed at creating a hostile environment that breeds atrocities, this factor should still be considered. Another example pertains to the Bosnian Genocide where Judge Florence Mumba reprimanded Kunarac, stating, "You abused and ravaged Muslim women because of their ethnicity, and from among their number, you picked whomsoever you fancied on a given occasion . . . By your natural authority [among the soldiers] you could easily have put an end to the women's suffering."[120] These words indicate that Kunarac, even though he committed many of the rapes himself, created an environment for the mass rapes to occur and even encouraged it. If the perpetrator egged the civilian population to commit the crimes, then that is a red flag against them alerting the judges that this was indeed part of a well-constructed plan.

4.2.3. Presence of military personnel

While the circumstances of the second factor need not be created by military or official state authority figures, the third factor requires the presence of military personnel. As suggested in the previous paragraph, military personnel have the weapons and means to stop atrocities. If they stand idly by in an immediate proximity where they can witness the sexual violence and choose not to react, they implicitly convey their approval of the crimes. During the Bosnian Genocide, one victim, identified as Witness A, was interrogated and brutally raped. This occurred in the presence of a Serbian soldier named Anto Furundzjia, who did not commit the rape himself. Nonetheless, like Jean-Paul Akayesu, even though Anto did not rape the victim, his presence and lack of doing anything to stop the rape, was enough to charge him with various crimes, including rape.[121] One of the variations of Milgram's experiment included a person in a gray lab coat and observed how the presence of an authoritative figure - whether or not he even gave orders - encouraged the test subject to carry out harming another person.[122]

Between the three above factors, the easiest for the prosecution to prove would be the first factor since it requires evidence of direct orders to commit sexual violence from authoritative figures. Such commands are often in writing, strengthening the prosecution's case.

---

[119] José E. Alvarez, 'Crimes of State/Crimes of Hate: Lessons From Rwanda' (1999) 24 *Yale J. Int'l L.* 365, 424-425.

[120] *See* Press Release, Presiding Judge Florence Mumba, Judgement of Trial Chamber II in the Kunarac, Kovac and Vukovic Case (22 February 2001) <http://www.icty.org/sid/8018>.

[121] Prosecutor v. Furundzija, IT-95-17/1 P 185 (Trial Judgment) (10 December 1998).

[122] Milgram, *supra* note 102, at 16.

4.2.4. *Rape as a "spectacle"*

Rape as a "spectacle" means that the rape, as a tool of genocide, was rarely an act committed privately. These rapes, viewed and talked about, were not shameful acts within the community of the perpetrators. They were bragged about. Various witnesses were present. In fact, the hostile party's women would calmly gaze at deviant sexual acts. MacKinnon states in the next line that the sexual violence was done to "shatter a society, to destroy a people."[123] Aside from the obvious humiliation that women endured, the rape "spectacle" was also a cruel tactic to humiliate men. The "strategy" was used to "destroy" the "morale and will" of men.[124] This was particularly true during the Bosnian Genocide, where the perpetrators aimed to send a message to the Muslim men that they cannot protect their women.[125] Therefore, genocidal rape, in addition to the physical and emotional pain it causes women, weakens the male population by destroying their ability to fight back.

4.2.5. *Pattern of behaviour*

The fifth factor calls for the use of circumstantial evidence. If there were not an abundance of witnesses, then it would be unfair to still find an individual guilty of rape as a crime against humanity. Rape as a "spectacle," the previous factor, aids immensely in establishing the pattern of behavior since the atrocious acts were executed publicly, demanding eyewitnesses and possibly showing a pattern. If the prosecutor is able to prove to the Court that the perpetrator(s) had a pattern of committing various crimes, and then following them with the rapes of women, this can definitely be a strong factor. This pattern can also aid courts in deducing whether rape was incident to the genocide or a means of advancing the genocide. Furthermore, one can also look to see if there were camps where women were detained or slavery was going on. Slavery as it pertains to women strongly suggests sexual abuse.

4.2.6. *Uniform dress*

The sixth factor is fairly simple to show, but it has its fair share of limitations. If a man commits rape while in his military uniform for example, he is acting on behalf of the state or hostile party. However, he may very well be wearing his uniform, drinking at a bar, and decide to rape a woman who just happens

---

[123] MacKinnon, *supra* note at 48, at 12.

[124] Debra Bergoffen, *Contesting the Politics of Genocidal Rape: Affirming the Dignity of the Vulnerable Body* (Routledge, New York 2012) 62.

[125] *Id.*

to be from the particular group that is the focus of the genocide.[126] It would not be appropriate to charge this individual with a crime against humanity.[127] Instead, this is a crime that is better left to the sovereign state to prosecute. That is why it is important to look at the totality of the circumstances with this factor, such as taking into account the seventh factor.

4.2.7. Derogatory words

The seventh factor can provide powerful evidence that the victims were singled out because of their identity. The perpetrators were not just raping any women; they were out to rape the victimised group, using terminology to degrade them. For example, in *Akayesu*, the Tutsis were labeled "*Inyenzi*" meaning "cockroach." Radios in the region would broadcast propaganda to "kill the cockroaches."[128] Another example of sexual violence was when Armenian Christian women were stripped naked and forced to dance in front of the Turkish gendarmes as they called them "infidel beauties" referring to their religion and a "bunch of [...] sluts" among other names.[129] Even the simple act of just uttering the woman's identifiable group during the course of the sexual violence already provides plenty of evidence as to why she is specifically targeted. Since the campaign of genocide encourages such vulgar name-calling, perpetrators do so without any shame. This lends itself to abundant trial testimony for this factor.

4.2.8. Forced impregnation or intent and knowledge to kill with sexual violence

Finally, the eighth factor just requires enough evidence to show that women were systematically raped and kept in custody until they gave birth to the children of the hostile party. Or, there needs to be evidence to show that the perpetrators were ordered to kill through the act of rape or immediately thereafter. It is possible that in some genocides, this factor is not even present. If the goal is not to impregnate by force, or to kill in the process of rape, then this factor need not be considered.

Analysing these factors and how heavily they weigh in the case will help draw the fine line between when numerous acts of rape actually fall under the term "genocide." This test relates to the existing jurisprudence because nearly

---

[126] Interview with Judge Scott Gordon (18 October 2013).
[127] *Id.*
[128] Monroe, *supra* note 76, at 356.
[129] Balakian, *supra* note 1, at 237.

all of the factors are drawn from judgments, and they strengthen the famous international humanitarian laws already in place for decades. Furthermore, a balancing test, as opposed to an elements test, is more appropriate in a genocidal rape context. The reason is simple: all factors may not be present in all genocides, and if one factor appears to be very weak in a particular case, a judge should have the liberty to assess other stronger evidence illustrated in another factor that may conspicuously point to genocidal rape. Each factor can mitigate or aggravate whether or not the rape was a tool of the genocide.

The 8-factor balancing test is important to use because when rape goes unpunished, it is an injustice to all women. But when rape as a tool of genocide goes unpunished, it is an injustice to humanity. The intent in the latter lies in completely destroying a particular group based on inherent traits or beliefs. Therefore, recognising systematic rape and prosecuting the perpetrators is the only right course to take.

4.3. Victim Support

As seen earlier in the Former Yugoslavia tribunals, rape victims are referred to with numbers or letters when testifying on the record. When a rape victim comes forward, steps must be taken to ensure her protection. Moreover, cultural differences complicate this. When drafting a statute, it is important to word the language with enough fluidity that it can be applied to victims from different national and cultural backgrounds - from the most conservative to the most socially liberal. Interestingly, the societal background of the victim is a large component in this, not that of the perpetrator. In some ways, the culture of the victim can present a challenging situation for her. Some are even very ashamed to face their own communities.[130]

The importance of this comes with the idea that if victims are not safeguarded, they are less likely to come forward with the story. She may fear rejection by her own family. This was seen in the case of the Bosnian Genocide where the women were forced to give birth to children. One such study in the United States showed that rape shield laws helped increase reporting by victims.[131] If these sexually violent crimes remain unreported, even if the perpetrators get charged with murder, torture, and various other crimes, the utilisation of rape in their systematic destruction goes undetected.

---

[130] Cohen, *supra* note 30, at 158.

[131] Cassia Sophn and Julie Horney, *Rape Law Reform: A Grassroots Revolution and Its Impact* (The Plenum Series in Crime and Justice, Plenum Press New York 1992) 88.

5. Conclusion

> "The real complaining party in this trial is civilization." – Justice Robert H. Jackson[132]

Genocide is a loaded term. Rape on its own is a murky concept and can, like genocide, be difficult to prosecute. When rape becomes a tool as part of a systematic destruction in genocide, it becomes easy to get lost in a legal labyrinth.

Especially in the context of genocide, women and their bodies have been perversely utilised to the advantage of the genocide. Therefore, it is more significant to analyse those crimes, piece the puzzle together, and see the whole picture: that the rape, death or not, pregnancy or not, resulted in the advancement of genocide. Still, it is important to look at all sides. In talking about the rights of women, the rights of the victims, the rights of humans, one must also not ignore the fact that the defendant has rights.[133]

Genocide trials have a long duration with multiple defendants and require a significant amount of evidence, since the crimes are so severe, often intricate, and occur over long period of time. The accused parties face serious sentences. The punishment and sentencing of the perpetrators is not an easy task for international judges to undertake.[134] The identity of the perpetrator, the number of rapes he committed, and the environment in which the crime was committed are just some of the issues a judge must consider.[135] While the majority of the Nazi defendants during the Nuremberg trials received prison sentences, some were sentenced to death by hanging.[136] However, nowadays, many countries have banned the death sentence.[137] In fact, Article 24 of ICTY statute explicitly states that sentencing must be "limited to imprisonment."[138]

---

[132] United States Supreme Court Justice Jackson, who was a prosecutor in the Nuremberg Trials, voiced this famous line in his opening statement. King, Jr., *supra* note 39, at 335.

[133] Amos Guiora, Professor at S. J. Quinney College of Law, University of Utah, "Southwestern Law School SBA Presents: Global Perspectives on Counterterrorism: Detention, Targeted Assassinations, Intelligence Gathering and Information Sharing" (5 March 2012).

[134] Interview with Scott Gordon, *supra* note 71.

[135] *Id.*

[136] Ellis Washington, 'The Nuremberg Trials: The Death of the Rule of Law (In International Law)' (2003) 49 Loy. L. Rev. 471, 487.

[137] Howard S. Levie 'The Statute of the International Tribunal for the Formal Yugoslavia: A Comparison with the Past and a Look at the Future' (1995) 21 Syracuse J. Int'l L. & Com. 1, 25.

[138] Statute of the International Criminal Tribunal for the former Yugoslavia, S.C. Res. 827, U.N. SCOR, U.N. Doc. S/RES/827 (1993).

It further gives discretion for the judges to decide the sentencing.[139] Similarly, ICTR mirrors that same phrase in Article 22.[140]

Since this article focuses strictly on rape with the knowledge that the perpetrator did it in furtherance of the genocide, his sentence should vary based on the amount of rapes he committed (ie, if he committed four rapes with four different victims and each sentence was a five year imprisonment, he would receive a twenty year prison sentence). This was my original idea but it had two major flaws: 1) It would be difficult to know the exact amount of women the perpetrator had raped and 2) Since the sentence is actually punishing for the act of rape with the knowledge of advancing the genocide, the number of acts one individual committed does not really matter.

Sentencing can also warrant a discussion about evidentiary issues. It would be unjust to issue a harsh sentence when there is not an overwhelming amount of evidence. The written judgments of these trials show how crucial the witness testimony is. At times, there are no witnesses to the sexual violence and the victim does not come forward, it can be almost impossible to charge the perpetrator with the crime. Moreover, if the victim dies from the rape, the evidence dies with her, unless a witness comes forward. Isolated incidents and random rapes without any knowledge of the planned genocide should not be considered. Circumstantial evidence can help alleviate some of these situations. For instance, as mentioned earlier, if there are patterns of wrecking villages, raping women, and murdering the population only to move on and repeat with another village, then it might be enough.

Still, sentencing occurs after the crime is executed which means the international world failed to prevent or halt the genocide at its inception. While it is possible for the women who did survive through the rapes to seek remedies, deterrence is a mightier weapon to combat treacherous crimes.[141] Both the victims and witnesses, as painful as it may be, as better it would be to forget, ought to record the every detail of the crimes.[142] To remember, to

---

[139] *Id.*

[140] Statute of the International Criminal Tribunal for Rwanda, S.C. Res. 955, Annex, U.N. Doc. S/RES/955/Annex (1994).

[141] In *Kadic v. Karadzic*, 70 F.3d 232 (2d Cir. 1995), rape victims in the Bosnian Genocide, using the Alien Tort Claims Act of 1789, successfully brought action against Radovan Karadzic in Manhattan, New York.

[142] My grandfather's mother, Mary Semerdjyan, was living in Turkey and attending school there. She and all other Armenians were forbidden to speak Armenian. Threatened by the gendarmes that they would have their tongues cut off if they spoke Armenian, Mary eventually forgot her native language. She would often share stories of the Armenian Genocide, but if someone spoke Armenian in her presence, she would get visibly upset. In some ways, the Young Turks successfully destroyed a part of her identity. Aghavni Jembelyan, my grandmother's mother, was a little girl when she witnessed a gendarme behead her father. Interview with Manvel Semerdjyan, son of Armenian Genocide survivor (Glendale, California, 26 October 2013).

document, and to prosecute can help deter these crimes in the future.[143] If perpetrators know that they will face severe consequences if caught, they are less likely to commit the crimes. Further, when the rape is included in an international law as a crime against humanity accelerating the objective of the genocide, hopefully, it will make the perpetrators think twice. Countries need to stand by one another. Before carrying out the Holocaust, Hitler did not worry that the world would react so quickly to his imminent crime, stating, "Who, after all, speaks today of the annihilation of the Armenians?"[144]

The above proposed balancing test is not perfect—but it is a start. Once international courts and tribunals can interpret the fine line between rapes that occur simultaneously at the time of genocide and rapes that are executed in furtherance of genocide, perpetrators will be punished leaving victims with some sense of comfort. In addition to experiencing the numerous horrors of genocide, raped women carry physical and emotional scars, deserving of recognition and justice that the balancing test will provide.

---

[143] As a junior at the University of California, Berkeley I combined my love for theater and human rights, producing, directing, and playing one of the characters in Lorne Shirinian's "Exile in the Cradle." Theater has the powerful magic to transport an audience and compel them to feel what the victims suffered. I donated the ticket proceeds to Darfur, in hopes of that it would help stop the conflict in Africa.

[144] Louis P. Lochner, *What About Germany?* (Dodd, Mead, & Company, New York 1942) 2

This a (Wo)Man's World: Reforming UK Equal Pay

Victoria Hooten[1]

This article provides a examines the current state of UK equal pay law and provides a comprehensive overview of the current problems women face in gaining equal pay to their male comparators, with a reform proposal for the UK government in order to address the problem of the UK pay gap. The article first sets out the manifest issues that can be seen in the equal pay statistics (including a comparison of the UK pay gap with other states), then assesses the case law that has arisen under the Equality Act 2010 and composes an evaluation in relation to a) women bringing equal pay claims in the first place and b) women actually succeeding in equal pay claims. The article then provides a critical analysis of reforms previously proposed by academics (and those implemented by other states), The article closes with suggestions for the best reform route for UK legislation. The value of this article is its original contribution in providing an up-to-date analysis on the status of equal pay, with a reform proposal which would suit the values of contemporary society.

Keywords: Equal Pay, Employment Law, Sex Discrimination, Equality Act 2010, *Armstrong v Newcastle upon Tyne NHS Hospital Trust*, Equal Pay Act 1970, ECHR.

1. Introduction

This article argues the need for UK equal pay reform in three parts. The first part shall look at the barriers to bringing a claim, the second assesses the barriers to succeeding in the claim, and the third part suggests viable reform routes for equal pay and proposes the best option.

---

[1] LLM Research Candidate, University of Manchester School of Law.

The Office of National Statistics released a report in 2013 that showed the UK pay gap is hovering close to the 20% mark, with men being paid on average £13.60 an hour and women £12.24.[2] The pay gap for full-time workers has risen from 9.5% in 2012 to 10% in 2013.[3] In 2011 Eurostat compared the gender pay gap of the EU member states, the UK was seventh with the highest pay gap with 20.1% (the highest being 27.3% in Estonia). Of even more concern is the absence of successful equal pay claims in the UK: the Equality and Human Rights Commission (hereafter 'EHRC') noted that less than 1% of equal pay claims are successful.[4] These statistics suggest that the law is in need of reform to bring the gender pay gap down and to make the equal pay provisions more accessible and efficient.

Equal pay claims are lengthy processes, with an average tribunal of around 229 weeks, whereas a working time tribunal is only 27.[5] It could be argued that equal pay claims are more complex, but that does not mean that the legislator should not look towards improving this issue. It has been noted "Proceedings take too long, involve too many hearings and are overly complex"[6].

2. Barriers to Bringing a Claim

In this section I will discuss the issues a complainant faces when bringing a claim. The main hurdle to overcome in these claims is choosing a comparator: "a higher paid employee of the opposite sex who is employed in the same establishment or by an associated employer, or by a different establishment in Great Britain at which common terms and conditions are observed generally or on an employee class basis".[7] The comparator also needs to do 'like work', 'work rated as equivalent' and 'work of equal value'. These headings are separate; a complainant only chooses one. Most complainants choose 'like

---

[2] Office of National Statistics, Annual Survey of Hours and Earnings http://www.ons.gov.uk/ons/rel/ashe/annual-survey-of-hours-and-earnings/2013-provisional-results/info-ashe-2013.html accessed on 21.02.14.

[3] Office of National Statistic, Annual Survey of Hours and Earnings (Provisional Results) < http://www.ons.gov.uk/ons/dcp171778_335027.pdf> accessed on 04.03.2014.

[4] Equality and Human Rights Commission, *Response of the Equality and Human Rights Commission to 'The Equal Pay Audits Further Consultation' (May 2013).* Available to download at <www.equalityhumanrights.com>accessed on 21.02.14.

[5] Ministry of Justice 'Tribunal Statistics Quarterly' Jan-Mar 2013 available to download at: < https://www.gov.uk/government/publications/tribunal-statistics-quarterly-and-annual-jan-mar-2013-2012-13> accessed on 21.02.14.

[6] Stephen Taylor and Astra Emir, 357. Emphasis added.

[7] Stephen Taylor and Astra Emir, 340.

work' because it is the easiest option to prove, being the broadest option and the option that will generally apply to all plausible cases.[8]

2.1. Non-use of Hypothetical Comparators

The comparator has to be a physical, existing person. [9] Other than this requirement, a female may choose anyone she wishes to compare herself with.[10] This is so employers cannot simply employ 'token males' to stop equal pay claims.[11] Barnard notes how hypothetical comparators would complicate and lengthen equal pay claims as they would involve industry-wide investigations and analysis, but also notes how the non-use of hypothetical comparators seriously disadvantages women in typical gender roles such as cleaning or catering who may not have a male comparator.[12] As useful as hypothetical comparators may be to rectify the issues above, it would be unfair to employers because of possible abuse of the system. It would also elongate and complicate proceedings when the focus should really be on simplification.

2.2. Problems with 'Like Work'

There is no strict definition of 'like work', but s.65 (2) and (3) of the Equality Act 2010 set out that the jobs must be at least broadly similar and have no differences of practical importance. To assess this the court must look at the nature and extent of any differences as well as the frequency.[13] The courts tend to ignore pedantic differences, demonstrated by the case of *Capper Pass Ltd v Lawton*[14] where it was made clear that the practical undertaking of the job is more important than a job title or job description. Selwyn provides examples of when work will be considered 'like'[15], such as different contractual duties (like compulsory overtime) which may only occur infrequently. This will not be a bar to an equal pay claim (as a company may use means other than greater pay to reward such actions)[16], as per *Electrolux v Hutchinson.*[17]

---

[8] Stephen Taylor and Astra Emir, 340.
[9] C Barnard, *EU Employment Law*, (4th edn, Oxford University Press 2012), 303.
[10] *Pickstone v Freemans Plc* [1989] AC 66.
[11] *Pickstone v Freemans.*
[12] C Barnard, at 303.
[13] Equality Act 2010, s.65.
[14] *Capper Pass Ltd v JB Lawton* [1976] IRLR 366 EAT.
[15] Astra Emir, *Selwyn's Law of Employment* (17th Edn, Oxford University Press 2012), 186-187 (points 5.23 to 5.30).
[16] Astra Emir, 186 (point 5.26).
[17] *Electrolux Ltd v Hutchinson* [1976] IRLR 410 EAT.

2.2.1. The rule for like work does not take into account sex discrimination that may affect the delegation of work.

The main problem with UK Equal Pay law is that it does not strive to settle inequality by changing outdated and sexist views of society and employers about the working role of women. An equal pay claim may open the door to possible wider scenarios of discrimination that an employment tribunal will ignore. For example, in *Eaton Ltd v Nuttall*[18], a man was responsible for handling items of a greater value, so any mistake on his part would result in more severe consequences. His higher pay was ruled to be justifiable. This seems fair, but if it were the *only* difference between the man and woman it would seem (for the advancement of equality) that a court should ask why the woman could not have the opportunity to handle items at the same level as the male. In *Noble v David Gold & Son (Holdings) Ltd*[19] men were paid more than the women who worked under the same employment simply because they had the job of lifting and unloading whereas women were sorting and labelling goods. It would be beneficial to equality if the courts would question 'why could women not do what men were doing?'. Women may be just as able to lift boxes; it promotes a very unhealthy and out-dated view of gender roles to assume they cannot, yet if such a view is accepted by a tribunal or court, this inequality of job distribution will remain unrectified.

This also highlights undervalue of typical 'women's work' (such as catering), which is something equal pay law does not attempt to fix. It has been noted by the Fawcett Society that employers need to increase the value they attach to women's work.[20]

It seems disadvantageous to equality that an employer may not be the subject of an equal pay claim by merely dividing responsibility in a discriminatory manner. There should be some mechanism that prompts investigation into any possible discrimination that may arise within the sphere of an equal pay claim; with the possibility that an employer may also have to face a sex discrimination claim afterwards.

2.2.2. The law does not take into account the demands of family roles.

The Fawcett Society refers this to as the 'motherhood penalty'.[21] Selwyn[22]notes that although working different times does not necessarily

---

[18] *Eaton Ltd v J Nuttall* [1977] IRLR 71 EAT

[19] *Noble v David Gold & Son (Holdings) Ltd* [1980] IRLR 252 CA

[20] The Fawcett Society Website, <http://fawcettsociety.org.uk/equal-pay/>, see heading 'What do we want to see happen?' accessed on 21.02.14.

[21] The Fawcett Society Website at n.20.

[22] Astra Emir at 187.

preclude an equal pay claim, an employer may pay males more favourably if they work a 24/7 rotating shift as per *Blackburn v Chief Constable of West Midlands Police*[23] even though this could potentially be unfair for women with children who are unable to work those type of hours.[24] The employment appeal tribunal in the aforementioned case stated: 'The assumption appears to be that the employers should [...] ensure that women and men on equal work are paid the same. That is not what the law requires[25]', which is obviously very concerning.

Canada faced the same issues with their equal pay legislation[26] in the 1970s and 1980s, which was not too dissimilar to the UK model as it stands now. Canadian wage differences were due to "the crowding of women into a narrow range of occupations" due to lack of domestic convenience in higher paying jobs[27] as well as non-enforcement of legislation (a problem faced by the UK when one examines equal pay statistics), and segregation in the workplace (an aforementioned issue with the UK model).[28] In section three I will discuss the action of Canada's legislature in combatting this, which may be helpful for a UK model. At the very least, UK judges should be mindful of family roles whilst they are interpreting the provisions of the Equality Act.

2.2.3. The 'All or Nothing Approach'

If a case is not strong enough to show 'like work', the tribunal does not aim to ensure proportionate pay differences, regardless of how disproportionate or unfair the pay gap may be between the complainant and comparator is. This can be illustrated by *Maidment and Hardacre v Cooper & Co.*[29] This issue was noted as a reason to reform the law by Darren Newman[30]. Awarding proportional pay is more in line with the spirit of equal pay; women should

---

23 *Blackburn v Chief Constable of West Midlands Police* [2009] IRLR 135 .

24 Astra Emir at 187.

25 *Chief Constable West Midlands Police v Blackburn* Appeal No. UKEAT/0007/07/MAA

26 Canadian Human Rights Act 1985, Part 1 (11).

27 Roberta Edgecombe Robb, 'Equal Pay for Equal Value: Some Issues & Policies' (1987) 13 Canadian Public Policy/ Analyse de Politiques 445, 447.

28 D.M. Shapiro and M. Stelcner, 'The Persistence of the Male-Female Earnings Gap in Canada, 1970-1980: The Impact of Equal Pay Laws and Language Policies' (1987) 13 Canadian Public Policy / Analyse de Politiques, 462.

29 *Maidment and Hardacre v Cooper & Co (Birmingham) Ltd* [1978] IRLR 462, issue noted by Michael Rubenstein in 'Equal Pay, UK Equal Pay Law' (2013) Discrimination Guide 2013, Equal Opportunities Review <http://www.eordirect.co.uk/Default.aspx?id=1163506&sq=UK,comparator,equal,pay> accessed 06.03.14.

30 Darren Newman, 'Repeal the Law on Equal Pay', (2012) 223 Equal Opportunities Review, < http://www.eordirect.co.uk/Default.aspx?id=1166317&sq=UK,comparator,equal,pay> accessed on 07.03.14.

not be underpaid because of their gender status. It is fair to expect employers to pay employees according to their worth. An employee who knows they are worth more than they are being paid is likely to lack motivation, which will eventually create cost for the employer.

What happens when a female is paid equally but should be paid more?[31] In *Evesham v North Hertfordshire Health Authority*[32] the complainant rightly deserved higher pay (due to the longevity of her service), but she could only claim for equal pay to her comparator, who had been on the job less time than her. She argued she should be paid what the comparator would be paid, if he had been in his post six years. The case was dismissed. This does not seem to appeal to the spirit of equal pay, equal pay law is meant to prevent women getting paid less than they should be. This is exactly what *Evesham* permitted.[33]

2.3. Problems with 'Work Rated as Equivalent'

A complainant may choose a comparator who is graded the same as her in job evaluation schemes, which are used by employers to determine pay rates. The main schemes used in equal pay cases are those that objectively score employees on a variety of factors such as 'skill' 'effort' and 'responsibility'.[34] These cases are more complex, as the work of the complainant and comparator may be entirely different in nature, but a job evaluation scheme has suggested they should be on the same level of pay.[35]

2.3.1. Objectivity and Unreliability of Job Evaluation Schemes.

Honeyball and Bowers note that the job evaluation looks at the jobs that are being undertaken and not really the workers who fill them. They suggest these types of schemes should only be a foundation to work from; they should not be decisive, as a more subjective assessment of individuals should also occur.[36] A complainant cannot challenge these schemes unless there is some

---

[31] Honeyball and Bowers, *Textbook on Employment Law* (11TH Edn, Oxford University Press (2010), 279.

[32] *Evesham v North Hertfordshire Health Authority* [2000] IRLR 257.

[33] For the full facts of Evesham see Rubenstein 'Equal Value update' (1999), 88 Equal Opportunities Review.<http://www.eordirect.co.uk/Default.aspx?id=1067730&sq=evesham,equal,pay> accessed on 07.03.14.

[34] Stephen Taylor and Astra Emir, 343 (exhibit 18.3).

[35] Stephen Taylor and Astra Emir, 342.

[36] Honeyball and Bowers, 282.

obvious flaw with them or they have an error.[37] Considering how important these schemes are for equality, it is quite evidence how unfair they are - it would seem natural to assume *any* problem should be addressed; especially as minor problems may create major differences. In *Springboard Sunderland Trust v Robson*[38] the claimant was given a score of 400 on their job evaluation and appealed the scheme so it was amended to 410, which was enough to put her on an equal pay as her chosen comparator. Simpson notes that even though clearly discriminatory schemes can be challenged, "those embodying disguised weighting in favour of jobs mainly or exclusively done by men" can satisfy the law.[39] The Equal Opportunities Commission (now the EHRC) has issued guidance on good practice when undertaking a job evaluation scheme, such as (1) having gender balanced parties in the process (i.e., job analysts should not all be male), (2) ensuring that no aspect of a job is left out (such as a caring quality which may be in favour of women), (3) not overemphasising factors predominantly male in nature (such as strength).[40] These are all useful suggestions but they would need strong enforcement to really make a difference, so there is a possible need for reform regarding the competence and powers given to the EHRC which should be able to enforce, rather than implore employers to follow their guidance.

2.3.2. A scheme in the employee's favour may not be mandatory

There is some discrepancy among UK courts as to whether a scheme is mandatory once carried out. In *O'Brien v Sim-Chem Ltd*[41], the House of Lords said that, once a scheme had been implemented, then a decision could be made as to whether equal pay should arise— much in line with the EU principle of equal pay for equal work.[42] However, in *Arnold v Beecham Group Ltd*[43], the HOL found that the parties would have to accept the scheme for it to be valid. In this case the employee could not file a claim merely because the employer found the scheme to be deficient. This is a clear weakness. An employer will not want to accept a scheme that is going to cost money; should

---

[37] Honeyball and Bowers, 283.

[38] *Springboard Sunderland Trust v Robson* [1992] IRLR 61

[39] R.C. Simpson, 'Job Evaluation and Equal Pay' (1981) 44 The Modern Law Review 334, 336.

[40] These ideas were noted by Muriel Robinson, 'Local Government & Equal Pay: Part 2' (2007) 76 Employment Law Bulletin 3. For more work of the Equal Opportunities Commission see: Equality and Human Rights Commission Website <http://www.equalityhumanrights.com/> accessed on 21.04.14 (EOC are now part of the Equality and Human Rights Commission).

[41] *O'Brien v Sim-Chem Ltd* [1980] IRLR 373 HL.

[42] Honeyball and Bowers, 283

[43] *Arnold v Beecham Group Ltd* [1982] IRLR 307 EAT.

it really be up to the employer to say that a scheme is valid? There are other problems with making schemes mandatory. For example, a risk of employers engaging in bribery or underhand tactics to make sure a scheme is in their favour, or deciding not to pursue a scheme at all (in which case a whole type of equal pay claim would be barred). There are ways around this though: the employer could be required to justify why they refused to implement the scheme. This would be just because there should be some reasonable expectation that they will abide by one if they decide to implement it. Another option would be to have an independent advisor analysing a scheme to decide whether it is appropriate.

2.4. Problems with 'Equal Value'

2.4.1. Restrictive and Lengthy

It must be noted that this heading can only be used if the 'like work' and 'work-related as equivalent' approaches cannot, as per *Hovell v Ashford and St Peter's Hospital NHS Trust*[44]. It is also important to note that these types of claims were only permitted after 1938 when the ECJ ruled in *Commission v UK*[45] that the UK should allow claims where the complainant demands a scheme to determine the equality of her work with a comparator. According to Taylor and Emir this allowed many more claims, which was one of the benefits of EU law.[46] This heading is essentially for women who cannot look to an evaluation scheme and cannot use a 'like work' comparator, but feel they are being treated unequally. To give all complainants the best opportunities, equal value should be an open choice regardless of whether the previous two are available.

These claims take so long because they involve experts[47] who must be independent and ACAS-approved. The expert undertakes an evaluation of the roles of the complainant and comparator. It is rare for the findings to be ignored.[48] The evaluation and report process can take months, which may be off-putting for women bringing a claim, especially with the recent tribunal changes whereby complainants have to pay legal costs.[49] The trial could also adjourn and allow the parties to commission their own evaluation so that both can submit a report and allow the tribunal to decide between the parties—this

---

[44] *Hovell v Ashford and St Peter's Hospital NHS Trust* [2009] IRLR 734.
[45] *Commission of the European Communities v United Kingdom* [1982] I.C.R 578.
[46] Stephen Taylor and Astra Emir, 345.
[47] Stephen Taylor and Astra Emir, 345.
[48] Stephen Taylor and Astra Emir, 345
[49] See 'Fees' section on the Justice website <
http://www.justice.gov.uk/tribunals/employment/claims> accessed on 10 Feb 2014.

is a less popular option due to the cost of independent commissioning and similar complexity to the expert process. Sarah Fredman has said that "*in either case the process is protracted and complex*".[50] There should be stringent time limits for the experts without putting excessive pressure on the investigation. There should also be a time limit on any challenges made to a report.

Currently, complainants have to inform ACAS of their intent to take their employer to a tribunal so that an advisor can work through the issues using a conciliation scheme.[51] ACAS believe this will save the stress, time, and money of a tribunal for complainants. While this requirement is fairly new and results are unknown, it may simply elongate an already lengthy process. The only concrete figures ACAS provide seem to be those in favour of the employer who will save money.[52] Even if the conciliation rules are helpful to an employee, the employer is not required to take part.[53] This is essentially just another bar to bringing an equal pay claim.

2.4.2. Governmental Apathy towards Equal Value

As mentioned above, this part of the legislation only came about as a result of an EU intervention,[54] and there have been suggestions that the law does not "*adequately reflect the 1982 decision*" of the ECJ.[55] Ellis noted that the "*Government's enthusiasm for this reform was non-existent*".[56] The drafting style of this legislation would be laughable were it not a serious detriment to achieving equality, a point noted by Napier.[57]

In fact, the law on equal value was so badly drafted that it was heavily criticised and had to be changed before the bill became law.[58] Issues still remain in this area. For example, an expert has no right to access the workplace, which could be a serious detriment to their findings and may further lengthen the investigation. An expert should be able to access whatever they need as long as the investigation does not disrupt business excessively. Additionally, experts cannot require anyone to give oral evidence, which poses another problem for investigation. The expert

---

[50] Sandra Fredman, 'Reforming equal pay laws' (2008) 37 Industrial Law Journal 193.
[51] ACAS website <http://www.acas.org.uk/index.aspx?articleid=4028> accessed on 28 Feb 2014.
[52] ACAS website at n.51 under 'What are the benefits of early conciliation?'.
[53] ACAS website at n.51 under 'What are the benefits of early conciliation?'.
[54] See Rubenstein 'Equal Value update'.
[55] HL Deb 05 December 1983 vol 445 cc882-90. Referenced in B.W. Napier, 41.
[56] Evelyn Ellis, 'A Welcome Victory for Equality' (1988) 51 The Modern Law Review 781, 783.
[57] B.W. Napier, 'Equal Pay and Equal Value' (1984) 43 The Cambridge Law Journal 40, 43.
[58] B.W. Napier, 43.

investigation needs to be taken more seriously—experts need a complete range of powers in order to conduct a meaningful investigation.

Another problem with the drafting of the law is the issue of whether there should be a term-by-term comparison in equal value claims, or whether contracts should be looked at as a whole to see if the complainant is treated less favourably. This issue arose in the case of *Hayward v Cammell Laird*[59] where the House of Lords stated it should be a matter of term-by-term comparison. Ellis believes that the court wanted to avoid judging the woman by the benefits she had been given because of her gender status. She may never have wanted better sick days, or days off for domestic duties; but she had them because she is a woman, though she might be happy to swap them for the same benefits as a male worker.[60] However, Ellis also notes that even after this case, the use of the word 'term' was a serious problem as it was left undefined; only one law lord attempted to define it and that definition has not been taken up by others.[61]

It has been established that the drafting of this particular provision was rushed and unfocused, with some evidence that this was the result of Parliament's apathy toward equal pay law. Shortly after the ECJ decision was made, an ex-Department of Employment official was reported to say that the Government was going to "*subvert as much as possible*" the decision, and would change equal pay law "*as little as possible*".[62] There is a need of reform to change this anti-equality culture in Parliament. Reform proposals would at least encourage meaningful communication about equal pay. Hopefully the recent large-scale equal pay claims will reduce the seeming apathy of the Government, especially as these claims are also affecting males—male staff at Trinity Saint David University have just won an equal pay claim.[63] The Government should, at the least, communicate with the EHRC in order to understand the issues; this may also promote a more equality-based culture for equal pay reform.

2.5. Conclusions

The foregoing shows that women struggle to bring a claim because of domestic roles, or because the discrimination may not fall under 'equal pay',

---

[59] *Hayward v Cammell Laird Shipbuilders (No.2)* [1988] 2 W.L.R. 1134.
[60] Evelyn Ellis, 782.
[61] Evelyn Ellis, 783.
[62] Reported in *The Guardian,* March 27th 1984. Referenced as in Dominic Byrne, 'An Unequal Right to Equal Pay' (1984) 11 Journal of Law and Society 247, 250.
[63] Steffan Rhys, '18 men win equal pay claim in landmark case against university', Wales Online 23 April 2014 <http://www.walesonline.co.uk/news/wales-news/university-wales-trinity-st-david-7023982> accessed on 5 May 2014.

or because of unreliability and possible rejection of job evaluations and the restrictive nature of 'equal value'. The next section investigates the problems that women may face, even if they overcome the difficulties mentioned above.

3. Barriers to Succeeding In a Claim

3.1. Employer Defences

An employer can engage in a number of defences against a claim. For example, by relying on a job evaluation scheme, by showing there is not 'like work', by proving that an equal value claim is not strong enough to succeed, and so forth.[64] However, the most contentious argument is the most widely used: that of the material factor defence. This is where the employer must demonstrate that there is a genuine and proper reason for paying a man higher than a woman, as long as it is proportionate to achieve a legitimate aim and does not involve sex discrimination.[65] This area of the law bears a number of concerns.

3.1.1. Two bites at the cherry

The 'material factor defence' may include such things as additional responsibility of the comparator[66], a higher degree of academic qualification[67], or longevity of service[68]. If an employer has already tried to argue a difference as a means to end a 'like work' comparison, this does not preclude the same difference being put forward for a material factor defence (as in *Christie v John. E. Haith Ltd)*.[69] This position has been criticised by Michael Rubenstein, who writes, "It is illogical that a difference in effort (or skill or responsibility) should not be sufficiently important to make two jobs of unequal value and yet the same difference should be treated as sufficient to negate the equal pay claim."[70] The more logical process would be to bar an employer from using

---

[64] Stephen Taylor and Astra Emir, 349.
[65] Astra Emir, 190 (point 5.43).
[66] *Waddington v Leicester Council for Voluntary Services* [1977] IRLR 32 as noted by Astra Emir, 190 (point 5.45).
[67] *Murray v East Lothian Regional Council* [1977] CLY 972 as noted by Astra Emir, 190 (point 5.45).
[68] Astra Emir, 191 (point 5.45).
[69] *Christie v John. E. Haith Ltd* [2003] IRLR 670.
[70] Michael Rubenstein 'Highlights October 2003' (2003) Industrial Relations Law Reports (accessed via Lexis Nexis); also cited by Honeyball and Bowers, 286.

the difference when the same argument failed to disprove the 'like work' defense.

3.1.2. Beyond the Personal Equation

In the case of *Clay Cross (Quarry Services) Ltd v Fletcher*[71] it was held that employers could only use this defence if the difference was within the 'personal equation' of the complainant and the comparator, so the difference had to be something that could clearly be proven between these two parties. Therefore, reasons personal to the employer could not be used in the 'material factor defence', such as market forces, i.e., the lack of a certain type of worker necessitating higher pay for the advancement of a headhunt. However, in *Rainey v Greater Glasgow Health Board*[72] Lord Keith noted that *all* circumstances of a case should be looked into, not just those beyond the personal equation.[73] Whilst this may be true, it is important to keep in mind the judgement of Lord Denning in *Clay Cross*, who noted that allowing market forces as a material difference would render equal pay statute useless, as "the door would be wide open. Every employer who wished to avoid the statute would walk straight through it."[74] Lord Denning believed that market forces as a defence would undermine the whole point of equal pay legislation, as women are more likely to take (or, firstly, be *offered*) a lower paid job simply because of their social subordination.[75] Peter Schofield has argued that the position set out by *Clay Cross* was unsustainable and agreed with Lord Keith of Kinkel that it was restrictive and that all the circumstances should be looked at for a proper analysis of the material difference.[76] It is not difficult to agree with this—all circumstances of the material difference should be looked at, but circumstances that do go beyond the personal equation should be *a* factor, not *the* factor. I suggest that any differences that do go beyond the personal equation should only be used to bolster circumstances within it. For example: an employer under the current law could argue 'I needed employee X and because this type of employee is rare I offered him more money', but under the suggested scheme the employer would have to argue 'I needed employee X because of his specialised qualifications/ experience, etc., *and*

[71] *Clay Cross (Quarry Services) Ltd v Fletcher* [1978] 1 WLR 1429.

[72] *Rainey v Greater Glasgow Health Board* [1987] AC 224.

[73] Hazel McClean, 'Equal Pay. The Employer's Defence' (1987) 46 The Cambridge Law Journal 224, 225.

[74] *Rainey v Greater Glasgow Health Board* [1987] AC 224 Lord Denning MR at 1433

[75] Hazel McClean, 225.

[76] Peter Schofield, 'Equal Pay. What's the difference?' (1987) 50 The Modern Law Review 379, 380.

these types of employees are rare so I had to pay him more'. This is much stronger justification and would be acceptable as a defence for unequal pay.

Fortunately, the effects of the *Rainey* judgement have not been too detrimental. *Benveniste v University of Southampton*[77] demonstrates the limitations of the use of market forces as a material factor. Because the factors affecting pay had ceased to exist before the claim began, the employer's defence failed.[78] Darren Newman has noted another limitation to this issue. The market factors still have to be proven by the employer,[79] as per *Lawrie v Rotherham, Doncaster and South Humber NHS Trust,*[80] where an employer failed to prove they had to pay a male more to recruit him. However, the use of factors beyond the personal equation still needs to be restricted in order to enhance the legitimacy of this defence.

3.1.3. Red-circling is still permitted.

Red-circling is the process of protecting an employee's pay when they are downgraded in some manner: in practice it freezes their pay. This aims to avoid a breach of contract or 'industrial unrest'.[81] New or existing employees will be paid a lower rate even though they are on the same level as an employee that has been 'red circled'. If discrimination has previously been a reason behind the higher pay of males, then red-circling will not protect an employer from an equal pay claim, as per *Snoxell and Davies v Vauxhall Motors Ltd*[82]. If the red-circling is for a genuine reason, such as age or illness[83], then it will be permitted as a material difference.

Red-circling, for the most part, is inherently unfair, as even if pay is frozen until others catch up, the red-circled employee will enjoy greater pay for a substantial amount of time. Ensuring that there is no breach of a contract via red-circling does not preclude the employer from raising the pay of current employees of equal worth, to ensure that all employees enjoy the same pay increase over time. This makes the issue more manageable and is surely easier (and cheaper) to calculate one set of pay increases without having to worry about 'frozen' pay of certain employees.

---

[77] *Benveniste v University of Southampton* [1989] IRLR 122 CA.

[78] Gerry R. Rubin, 'Equal pay - in the same employment - genuine material factor other than sex' (1989) Journal of Business Law 344.

[79] Brian Napier QC, 'Equal Pay in 2013' (2014) 246 Equal Opportunities Review < http://www.eordirect.co.uk/Default.aspx?id=1195253&sq=napier,equal,pay,2013> accessed on 7 May 2014.

[80] *Lawrie v Rotherham, Doncaster and South Humber NHS Trust* [2003] CqLR 934.

[81] Honeyball and Bowers, 289.

[82] *Snoxell and Davies v Vauxhall Motors Ltd* [1977] IRLR 123 EAT.

[83] Honeyball and Bowers, 290.

Red-circling was one of the main issues in the combined cases of *Redcar & Cleveland Borough Council v Bainbridge* and *Surtees v Middlesbrough Borough Council*[84] where it was argued that males should not have pay protection that afforded them greater pay than females just because a re-grading was arranged to settle inequalities already in place.[85] The issue was that the Councils were trying to stop inequality with further inequality, like trying to stop a fire with a bucket of diesel; it was reported, "the deal further perpetuated the inequality in salaries between women and men and was therefore illegal."[86]

All red-circling cases should be precluded from the material factor defence—why should female workers suffer inequality because the employer has decided to re-grade certain workers? Obviously there is the issue that the employer would have to pay out a substantial amount to other workers to bring them to an equal pay status with protected employees. However, referring back to the *Sainsbury's* case[87], the cost of a tribunal claim can be quite high. It could be argued that employers are setting themselves up for a fall if they allow unequal pay to persist after red-circling, as it will lead to employee unrest and perhaps a costly tribunal. It could even be argued that the tighter the rules are for equal pay, the less risk there is that an employer will face an expensive tribunal. Tighter laws would help breed an equal pay culture into employers, which is necessary to close the pay gap.

3.2. Burden of Proof

The black letter law of the *Equality Act* appears to place the burden on the claimant to show the facts of a pay difference by pointing to a suitable comparator. The burden then shifts to the employer to show a genuine defence; if they cannot then the claimant succeeds.[88] This seems simple and effective but the courts have not allowed the law to remain this way.

---

[84] *Redcar & Cleveland Borough Council v Bainbridge and Surtees v Middlesbrough Borough Council* [2008] IRLR 776.
[85] Honeyball and Bowers, 290.
[86] Katy Dowell, *Appeal Court makes landmark equal pay decision,* The Lawyer 29th July 2008. <http://www.thelawyer.com/appeal-court-makes-landmark-equal-pay-decision/134004.article> accessed on 21 Mar 2014.
[87] See *Sainsbury's Case*, Stephen Taylor and Astra Emir.
[88] Astra Emir, 193 ('Burden of Proof').

3.2.1. *The* Armstrong *Decision*

In the controversial decision of *Armstrong v Newcastle upon Tyne NHS Trust,*[89] the Court of Appeal held that an employer only has to justify a difference in pay if the complainant can show that it is tainted by indirect sex discrimination (an employer cannot justify direct discrimination).[90] This case is problematic for many reasons. It is in contrast to EU law, which states in *Brunnhofer v Bank der österreichischen Postsparkasse AG*[91] that unequal pay is precluded "whatever the mechanism, which produces such inequality, unless the difference can be justified".[92] There is no discrimination requirement. If Mrs. Armstrong's case had been decided in Luxembourg, she would not have had to show that the difference was tainted by sex discrimination; it would have been up to the employer to show that it was not. There is also nothing in the Equality Act[93] that suggests this is how the process should work, nor is there guidance in the statutory code of practice.[94]

The result of *Armstrong* is that it is difficult for women to bring claims at all if they cannot show that the difference has to do with gender.[95] Likewise, it may affect the complainant's free choice of comparator if they have to show that discrimination has taken place.[96] A woman could only really show that the difference in pay is generally detrimental to women by showing it is predominantly women that are affected[97], which could be difficult in typical women's work employment such as cleaning or catering. It is difficult to comprehend the logic in a system that requires an employee to prove discrimination when "*the relevant facts justifying the variation...will usually be within the employer's sole knowledge*".[98]

If the complainant does prove sex discrimination was at the heart of the difference, the employer is still not required to objectively justify the reason

[89] *Armstrong v Newcastle upon Tyne NHS Trust* [2006] IRLR 124.
[90] Iain Steele, 'Sex discrimination and the material factor defence under the Equal Pay Act 1970 and the Equality Act 2010' (2010) 39 Industrial Law Journal 264.
[91] Case C-381/99 *Brunnhofer v Bank der österreichischen Postsparkasse AG.*
[92] *Brunnhofer*, para 30. Emphasis added.
[93] Equality Act 2010, Chapter 3.
[94] Equality and Human Rights Commission, *Equal Pay: Statutory Code of Practice*, 2011 <http://www.equalityhumanrights.com/uploaded_files/EqualityAct/equalpaycode.pdf> accessed on 21 Feb 2014, pages 27–29.
[95] Stephen Taylor and Astra Emir, 351.
[96] Simon Deakin and Gillian S Morris, *Labour Law* (5th Edition, Hart Publishing (Oxford) 2009), 615 (point iv).
[97] Simon Deakin and Gillian S Morris, 624.
[98] A Lester, *Leading Counsel's Opinion on the Proposed Amendments to the Equal Pay Act 1970: European and Community Law* (Equal Opportunities Commission 1983), as cited by Dominic Byrne, 'An Unequal Right to Equal Pay' (1984) 11 Journal of Law and Society 247

for the difference.[99] This also stands in contrast to EU law. In *Enderby v Frenchay HA*[100] it was held that EU law "requires the employer to show that that difference is based on objectively justified factors unrelated to any discrimination on grounds of sex"[101] when there is a clear difference between female pay and male pay.

This is detrimental to the woman and supposedly 'helpful' to an employer[102] yet it might not be so, it may merely lengthen the case before the tribunal, resulting in more costs for the employer. If the employer could develop a defence, put it into play and have it accepted or rejected, the case would usually take less time. In addition, making the employer objectively justify the difference in pay the instant such a difference is established is the "only effective way to eliminate centuries of ingrained assumptions and practices leading to the systematic underpayment of women."[103] Steel has noted how this would shift the focus of equal pay legislation from sex discrimination to implementing fair wages. I disagree with Steel and believe that equal pay law is the realm in which these two focuses overlap, and therefore it should cater to both: impose fair wages and rid the workplace of sex discrimination.

The *Armstrong* decision could be seen as confusing the *impact* of lower pay with the *reasoning* of it[104]: the employee has to show that the reason for difference is tainted by sex discrimination. They do this by showing that women are consistently paid less than men. Yet this does not elucidate the reason, it demonstrates the impact of the reason. So the employer could be defending indirect discrimination (impact) when the reason was direct discrimination—which is indefensible. The law is therefore illogical, complex, and unfair. It has been seen as 'regrettable' that Parliament did not take time to clarify the law when enacting the Equality Act.[105] It would have been logical and beneficial to re-instate the black letter law and denounce the law as found in *Armstrong*.

---

[99] Michael Rubenstein, *Armstrong Reconsidered,* Equal Opportunities Review, Issue 198, March 2010.
[100] *Enderby v Frenchay Health Authority* [1993] IRLR 591.
[101] *Enderby*, para 19.
[102] Stephen Taylor and Astra Emir, 351.
[103] Iain Steele, 'Sex discrimination and the material factor defence under the Equal Pay Act 1970 and the Equality Act 2010' (2010) 39 Industrial Law Journal 264.
[104] Iain Steele, *ibid.*
[105] Iain Steele, *ibid.*

4. General Reform Proposals

In this section I will look at reform proposals put forward by various academics, assessing their strengths and weaknesses and determining their viability in the UK. I will highlight three options available to a legislator.

4.1. Specific Changes for Equal Pay

In the body of this article I have highlighted changes that should be made to combat each problem I have discussed. Those are the minimum changes the Government should make to equal pay law, but more substantial reform is desirable.

4.2. Repealing Equal Pay Provisions

Under s.70 of the Equality Act women who cannot bring an equal pay claim (i.e., for lack of a male comparator) may use sex discrimination law to challenge unequal pay.[106] There have been suggestions that *all* equal pay cases should be brought under sex discrimination law. Darren Newman has advocated this approach to reform.[107] One reason for this is that the Equality Act did not help equal pay law, as it was only 'consolidating' and did not clarify the law.[108] It would be more beneficial to bring claims under sex discrimination, as this is based upon tort and not contract, therefore damages including psychological injury would be awarded (which may be more substantial than back pay with a six month time limit).[109] Newman notes that because the burden of proof now rests upon the claimant to show *discrimination* (as per *Armstrong*[110]), there is essentially no difference in the practice for bringing sex discrimination or equal pay.[111] Equal pay, as it stands, would only be a better process for the claimant if the black letter law were reinstated. I have argued this as a reform; if the Government followed this scheme, Newman's reform route would not be viable.

The advantages of this reform is that there would be no need to identify a real-life male comparator. Any such comparator would merely be further

---

[106] Stephen Taylor and Astra Emir, 360.
[107] Darren Newman, 'Repeal the law on equal pay' (2012) 223 Equal Opportunities Review < http://www.eordirect.co.uk/Default.aspx?id=1166317&sq=UK,comparator,equal,pay> accessed on 6 Apr 2014.
[108] Darren Newman, paragraph 1.
[109] Darren Newman, paragraphs 7 and 8.
[110] *Armstrong v Newcastle upon Tyne NHS Trust* [2006] IRLR 124.
[111] Darren Newman, paragraphs 9 to 11.

evidence in the claimant's favour that there has been discrimination.[112] There would also be no need to show equal work, again this would merely be further evidence of discrimination.[113] However, it is important to note that the burden to show these factors would still be quite high for the claimant to succeed. Just because there is no legal requirement to show a comparator/equal work does not mean there is no factual requirement (although there may be scope for a hypothetical comparator to be cited in such cases).[114]

This proposal would also correct any undervaluement of 'women's work', as it would allow for proportional pay to be enforced if equal pay could not be.[115] This is desirable in the UK, because it unjust that a woman's work may be worth 95% of the man's, yet her employer may only pay her 70%, and an equal pay tribunal may not rectify the inequality.[116] Newman also believes that the clarity this would bring to the law would address the issue of costly claims for employers.[117]

The problem with Newman's model is that it may be seen as trivialisation of equal pay if the provisions that specifically deal with it are deregulated. It also does not account for the larger need for the UK pay gap to be resolved by ensuring a culture of proactivity amongst employers. An enforcement of positive duties is needed to achieve that goal, which this reform proposal does not address.

4.3. Imposing Positive Equal Pay Duties

Sarah Fredman believes that the complaints-led model has been exposed as a weakness in UK equal pay law.[118] I have stated above that Canada had similar issues with their Equal Pay policy. Fredman notes how the Canadian 'Pay Equity Taskforce' believed the only way forward was an employer-duty based approach because the complaint-led system breeds "*uncertainty, tension and frustration*".[119] Fredman advocates a process whereby the employer must seek out and rectify inequality in the workplace.[120] This changes the onus of proof for complainants into a burden for the employers, which is arguably

[112] Darren Newman, para. 12.
[113] Darren Newman, para. 13.
[114] Stephen Taylor and Astra Emir, 360.
[115] Darren Newman, para. 13.
[116] Example given by Simon Deakin and Gillian S Morris, 623 (point iv).
[117] Darren Newman, para. 15.
[118] Sarah Fredman, 'Reforming Equal Pay Laws' (2008) 37 Industrial Law Journal193
[119] Pay Equity Taskforce and Departments of Justice and Human Resources Development Canada, Pay Equity: A New Approach to a Fundamental Right (2004) as cited by Sarah Fredman, available via <http://ywcacanada.ca/data/research_docs/00000052.pdf> accessed on 12 May 2014.
[120] Sarah Fredman, *ibid.*

desirable.[121] Fredman believes this would bring UK law more in line with EU provisions, which encourages member states to *ensure* prohibition of unequal pay.[122]

It is not advisable to follow a reform proposal because of the rhetoric of EU policy, but there is some merit to this system. If there is systematic appraisal of employee treatment, then *any* discrimination will be addressed (such as job segregation as well as pay).[123] Fredman believes this will change the habits and attitudes of employers and will create a co-operative culture for equal pay.[124] This reform style could save employers money by reducing the risk of widespread litigation that could result in increased wage expenditures; any changes would be systematic instead of imposed by a tribunal.[125] Also, this solution is less dramatic than Newman's idea; it is a top-up reform which bolsters the current law.

Fredman points out two challenges to this model. First is the need to ensure co-operation at all levels. Leaving equal pay in the hands of individuals clearly has not worked, so it will likely not work if the roles reverses and it is in the hands of the employer.[126] I suggest that a statutory body should be created, independent of any employer, to help create a communication platform between employers and employees. Switzerland and Canada both have an independent body to investigate equal pay compliance.[127] It was mentioned above that the Equality and Human Rights Commission should have extended powers—they should be able to enforce equal pay practice and investigate possible breaches so that initiation is not left entirely to the employer or individual employees.

This solution would also help the second issue with this model: the need to synchronise a positive duty with a complaints system so anything overlooked by the employer (purposefully or not) may be brought to the attention of tribunals.[128] An independent body could receive complaints if the positive duties of the employer are not in existence. This takes the full burden from the individual. It would also help with the unsure nature of the current law: an independent body would be able to recognise a claim that had a high possibility of success, so there would be less time wasted on frivolous claims and the success rate would increase.

---

[121] Stephen Taylor and Astra Emir, 357.
[122] Sarah Fredman, Part 4 (point 'A').
[123] *Ibid.*
[124] *Ibid.*
[125] *Ibid.*
[126] *Ibid.*
[127] The Swiss Body: The 'Federal Office for Gender Equality', See Gender Employment Workshop, 15. The Canadian Body: The Pay Equity Commission: < http://www.payequity.gov.on.ca/en/about/index.php> accessed on 5 May 2014.
[128] Sarah Fredman, Part 4 (point 'A').

Another issue that Fredman's proposal fails to address is that this system is open to defensiveness by employers. It is analogous to why corporate social responsibility is not legally enforced—a lack of will does not breed good results. If an employer is forced into equalising pay on a wide-scale basis, they may resort to other tactics to make sure their wage bill stays low (i.e., not employing as many women) or may cut costs in other areas that run afoul of other employment law principles. The answer to this problem may lie with the Swiss Government, who engineered an effective equal pay policy[129] that has been heralded by the European Union. Article 8 of the Federal Constitution states women and men should have equal pay of equal value in law and practice.[130] Switzerland's Government boldly announced they would only do business with companies that obeyed the law of equal pay.[131] To assess inequality levels a software tool was created (called 'LOGIB') that allows companies to check their compliance with equal pay law without cost.[132] Government-contracting businesses were given a grace period to rectify any problems, before the Swiss government would refuse to do business with them.[133] The Swiss government not only *pushes* employers towards equal pay implementation, it *pulls* them towards it using incentives such as a certificate of equal wage policy, contracts, and financial support.[134] The Swiss pay gap is still close to the UK's gap at around 18%, but it is early in the implementation of the current model, and the Swiss government vows to continue, claiming that "much has been done, a lot still remains".[135]

I believe this 'top-up' system is the best solution to the problems with equal pay law. It retains the current law, avoiding the need for an overhaul, but improves the law in significant ways. It provides a champion system for employers while giving employees the support they need to succeed with equal pay claims. The certificates of equal pay encourages companies to show they are 'diverse' and centred around equality in order to gain the best choice of employees.

---

[129] Megan Beyer, 'Next Stop: Equal Pay Day', The Huffington Post 04/03/14 <http://www.huffingtonpost.com/megan-beyer-/next-stop-no-more-equal-pay-day_b_5079489.html> accessed on 14 Apr 2014.

[130] Sylvie Durrer, Gender and Employment Workshop, *Equal pay for equal work or work of equal value: Swiss practices,* <http://www.ebrd.com/downloads/research/sustain/4durrer.pdf> accessed 14.04.14.

[131] Megan Beyer, *ibid.*

[132] Gender and Employment Workshop, 7.

[133] Megan Beyer, *ibid.*

[134] Gender Employment Workshop, 19.

[135] The 'Federal Office for Gender Equality', Gender Employment Workshop, 21.

5. CONCLUSION

This article highlights the need for change in the current system of equal pay. The law needs to be more sensitive to the traditional role of women when it comes to choosing a comparator, there needs to be some way to address wider discrimination that is revealed in equal pay claims, and the courts should be able to award proportionate pay if equal pay is not suitable. There should also be some way of ensuring efficiency of job evaluations, possibly by utilising the EHRC to enforce good practice and ensure that when job evaluation schemes are found to be unacceptable by the employer, that this is justifiably so and not merely because it would allow for a successful equal pay claim. It seems there is very little that can be done for equal value claims except to rewrite the legislation or issue guidance that will clarify ambiguities.

It is evident that the material difference defence leans too heavily in an employer's favour. It was also evident that the defence over complicates the burden of proof in an illogical manner; the black letter law should be followed. The range of factors that may be a material difference should be limited in order to give the employee a chance to succeed.

In respect to reform proposals, the idea of deregulating equal pay to allow sex discrimination claims to cover pay was rejected. Top-up reform would be better, as it would implement a new system of positive duties and rid the law of the complaints-based model. I have argued that the EHRC should be able to seek out and find inequality in the same way Swiss and Canadian authorities do, creating a hybrid whereby there are positive duties for an employer to ensure equal pay, but also a tribunal system to rectify cases when they do not. I have also noted how a champion-type system should be founded, whereby employers that do conform to equal pay should be heralded and recognised by the Government.

In Verrem: The Case That Changed the Course of Jurisprudential History

André M. Santamaria[1]

This paper addresses a frequent omission in the contemporary discussion of Natural Law Theory; it is often the case that when addressing it, academics and jurists focus on Fuller or Dworkin, and sometimes progress as far back as Aquinas, but seldom are the true roots of Natural Law Theory pursued. This paper offers the story of Marcus Tullius Cicero, expounding upon the great Roman lawyer's role in the trajectory and development of Natural Law Theory (which is arguably the foundation for the existence of all Western democracies and Republics). This paper argues that Cicero's victory in the trial known as In Verrem *changed the course of jurisprudential history due to the rise of the Cicero as a result of said victory, which permitted him to significantly influence Roman republican jurisprudence. Germaine to this paper's conclusion is the illustration of a nexus between modern Natural Law incarnations and the postulations of Cicero. In order to demonstrate that Cicero should be credited with the crafting of the first Natural Law Theory (in the systemic sense of the word theory), this discussion also incorporates an effort to identify similitude, or a cause-effect relationship, between Cicero's Natural Law Theory and its more modern forms.*

Keywords: Jurisprudence, Legal History, Natural Law Theory, Roman Jurisprudence.

---

[1] JD and International Law Certificate, Florida Coastal School of Law; undergraduate degree in International Relations from The Latin University of Costa Rica.

1. INTRODUCTION

There are many great legal traditions, and within them, many methods of pondering the law. Arguably the greatest of legal traditions is that incarnated by our own legal system, the Common Law. While jurisprudential philosophies may be employed to discuss the law in any system, anywhere in the world, one need look no farther than the United States of America to find the principal jurisprudential philosophies on full display, in full intellectual battle array. From the H.L.A. Hart versus Lon Fuller debate in the Harvard Law Review[2], to the regularly disparate rationale or reasoning offered by each of the Justices of the Supreme Court of the United States, the jurisprudential realm of this nation is awash with the debate between multiple jurisprudential modes of interpretation. Principal among them are Positivism and its primary foe, Natural Law Theory.

As alluded to above, many of the great legal minds often associated with Natural Law Theory are of a more modern bent, therefore it is not surprising that jurisprudential discussions often neglect certain historical contributors to Natural Law Theory. It may simply be in the interests of expediency that the focus of discussions on Natural Law Theory is most often centered around more recent theorists, such as Lon Fuller or his recent antecedents. After all, there is only so much time in a classroom setting and only so many pages in a jurisprudence textbook. In an effort to expand the discussion of Natural Law Theory towards a more historically encompassing scope and thereby do better justice to its founders, this paper will argue that Marcus Tullius Cicero's victory in the trial known as *In Verrem* changed the course of jurisprudential history due to the rise of the Cicero as a result of said victory, which permitted him to significantly influence the trajectory of Roman republican jurisprudence. Once the above has been demonstrated, Cicero will be concluded to have been the systemic founder of Natural Law Theory.

In order to prove the veracity of this paper's thesis, the discussion shall commence with a brief review of the late Roman Republic and its legal system so as to set the stage upon which the breadth of the events discussed here took place, after which the discussion will shift to a glancing overview of the life of Marcus Tullius Cicero so as to craft an understanding who he was, and why he came to believe in Natural Law theory. Subsequently, the discussion will move to an overview of the trial known as *In Verrem*, in which its factual background as well as historical outcome shall be briefly analyzed. Later, the focus will move towards Cicero's legacy as it relates to jurisprudence, and finally, this paper will conclude that Cicero's success

---

[2] *See* Hart, H. L. A. "Positivism and the Separation of Law and Morals" [Feb. 1958] Harv. L. Rev., Vol. 71, No. 4, 593-629, *See also* Fuller, Lon L. "Positivism and Fidelity to Law — A Reply to Professor Hart" [Feb. 1958] Harv. L. Rev. Vol. 71, No. 4, 630-672.

during and following *In Verrem* allowed for the creation of Natural Law Theory as we know it today.

2. CONTEXTUAL BACKDROP

There are many nexuses between Western societies of today and the late Roman republic. This becomes apparent when one considers the fact that the Roman Republic (not to be confused with the subsequent Roman Empire) was the first quasi-modern state; it contained borders, a defined political and legal system, governments resulting from regular elections, enduring institutions and bureaucracies, citizenship with corresponding rights and obligations, and even notions of due process.[3] It could be argued that the modern state, modern notions of due process and the rule of law, modern schools of philosophy and ethics, and even modern political parties all derive their origins from one or another faction of the Roman Republic's political dichotomy.

Discussing historical antecedents of the modern American political structure, George Anstaplo postulated that '[t]he greatest republic before the one founded in 1776-1789 is that of ancient Rome, the influence of which on the American founders may be seen in the language (including the names), the institutions, and even the architecture which come down to us from Eighteenth-Century America. Our founders also took from Rome warnings about how republican government can be subverted by military establishments and military successes. Caesarism was always something to be guarded against.'[4] If, in fact, the modern American Republic can be viewed as indirectly resulting from the Roman Republic, then it is no great stretch to accept that modern natural law theory is a direct result of Cicero's legal and political career specifically, as well as the pro-Republic faction of the Roman Senate in general (of which Cicero arguably went on to become the leader after his meteoric rise in stature following his triumph in *In Verrem*).[5]

While it is true that several of the great Greek philosophers of antiquity can be said to have 'planted the seed' that would blossom into Cicero's here-discussed natural law theory (particularly Socrates and Aristotle), and that therefore these Greeks were the first natural law theorists, the Roman Republic (largely due to Cicero's career long influence upon its politics) was the first place where the natural law was polished and formed into a

---

[3] Velleius Paterculus, *The Roman History*, trans. J. C. Yardley and Anthony A. Barrett (Cambridge, MA: Hackett Publishing, 2011), 19; *See Generally* Plutarch, *Fall of the Roman Republic* , trans. Rex Warner (New York, NY: Penguin Books, 1972) 311-361.

[4] George Anastaplo, "The Constitution at Two Hundred: Explorations" [1991] 22 Tex. Tech L. Rev. 967, 978.

[5] Marcus Tullius Cicero, *Political Speeches,* trans. D.H. Berry (New York, NY: Oxford University Press Inc., 2006) xii-xxx.

functioning theory rather than a disjointed series of postulations or principles.[6] Additionally, while neither Socrates nor Aristotle were more than academics (which is not meant derisively, but merely factually) Cicero was a legal scholar, a practicing lawyer, and eventually was elected Consul of Rome (the modern-day equivalent of co-president).[7] Therefore, the impact of Roman Republicanism, and of its political and jurisprudential happenings upon actuality, cannot be overstated.

2.1. The Late Roman Republic and Its Legal System

There are many institutional similarities between the late Roman Republic and the modern American republic. The Roman republican political system was one in which annual 'federal' elections were held.[8] Roman citizens would vote in groups called 'centuries' (not unlike tribal or loose familial units) which would then declare their support as a unit for a particular consular candidate. There were typically thirty-five centuries comprising the electorate.[9] Roman citizenship could be obtained by virtue of birth or by virtue of a term of service in the Legion. All citizens were given the right to vote in the annual elections, however it is noteworthy that, as there was no universal suffrage at the time, only men could be voting citizens[10][11] After the voting concluded, the resulting first and second placed candidates became Consuls.[12] Each was tasked with the equivalent of the executive governance of the state for that year, and each Consul was typically given the role of commander-in-chief of one half of the Republic's standing army.[13] During the Republican period, no Consul could stand for reelection for two consecutive terms.[14] More often than not, outgoing Consuls would be given, by the Senate, governorship of a lucrative province, both to reward them for their service and to entice them to

---

[6] *Id.*

[7] *Id.*

[8] "Roman Republic", <www.princeton.edu/~achaney/tmve/wiki100k/docs/Roman_Republic.html> accessed 6 October 2014.

[9] *Id.*

[10] Though it is worth noting that the women of the middle and upper classes did enjoy some legal protections to their person and status.

[11] *Id.*

[12] "How Rome Was Governed", <www.historylearningsite.co.uk/how_was_rome_governed.html> accessed 6 October 2014; *See also* <www.ancienthistory.about.com/od/romerepublic/qt/052611-How-the-Romans-Voted-in-the-Roman-Republic.html> accessed 6 October 2014.

[13] *Id.*

[14] *Id.*

respect the continuity of the republican institution of elections by not usurping power.[15][16]

While the Senate was a unicameral body, it was divided into two broad segments and therefore was not entirely conceptually distinct from a bicameral system (for example the British system which contains both the House of Lords and the House of Commons); the Senators (who, much like the historical British House of Lords, must be members of the aristocratic class) comprised the majority of the house, while the Tribunes of the Plebes (who, much like the historical British House of Commons, could be members of any enfranchised social class and were often from the working class) constituted the minority of the house.[17] The power of the Tribunes of the Plebes cannot be overstated though, they were often extremely influential due to their ability to 'make or break' certain senatorial coalitions with their significant voting bloc in the Senate.[18]

The Roman legal system contained a complex and advanced series of subject matter jurisdiction-specific Courts, and even had rules of evidence, as well as notions of procedural and substantive due process.[19] The Roman judiciary was an autonomous and self-contained branch of government which purported to hold all who fell within its jurisdiction to account.[20] All Roman citizens, of any class, were (theoretically at least) entitled to the same legal protections, and this fact would feature prominently in Cicero's legal argumentation.[21] Considering the complexity of the Roman political and legal structure, and its striking similarity to our own, it is less vexing to concede that a seemingly complex jurisprudential philosophy—like Natural Law Theory—could find its origins in the Roman republican political dichotomy of over 2000 years ago.

2.2. A Glancing View at the Life and Times of Marcus Tullius Cicero

While the Rome of Cicero's time was not as socially enlightened nor upwardly socially mobile as today's free-market societies, there are vestiges and insinuations of an ancient version of the 'American dream hinted at within the story of the life and times of the great lawyer. Cicero was a 'new man,'

---

[15] Such governorships were often very lucrative, and therefore rather successful at luring outgoing Consuls away from Rome immediately following their term.

[16] *Id.*

[17] *Id.*

[18] *Id.*

[19] Marcus Tullius Cicero, *Political Speeches,* trans. D.H. Berry (New York, NY: Oxford University Press Inc., 2006) xii-xxx; *See also* Gaius Julius Caesar, *The Civil War,* trans. John Carter (New York, NY: Oxford University Press Inc., 2008) viii-xlix.

[20] *Id.*

[21] *Id.*

which was in essence the Roman Republic's version of someone who in modern parlance may be said to be 'nouveau riche'; he hailed from an agricultural province of Rome and was not a member of the aristocracy by birth.[22] His family was, at most, upper-middle class by modern standards.[23] His struggle to overcome social prejudice, nepotism, and cronyism led to his view that certain universal laws apply to all, that they transcend social class, and that the value and nobility of the Roman republic lay in its rule-of-law nature (which, along with due process, was something that Cicero fought for during his entire career).[24]

Cicero was born 3 January, 106 B.C in Arpinum, a small rural town about seventy miles southeast of Rome.[25] After his childhood education and schooling in the foundational subjects (grammar and rhetoric, among other subjects), Cicero studied law under Mucius Scaevola, who was widely considered to be among the greatest lawyers of the day.[26] In Cicero's time, there were no law schools as there are now, instead, young academics would shadow and learn from mentors (usually practicing lawyers).[27] Towards the end of his teenage years, while still being mentored by Scaevola, Cicero regularly attended trials in furtherance of his legal education.[28] After a brief and half-hearted stint in the military at eighteen, Cicero studied the art of rhetoric in Greece under Apollonius Molon, a respected orator in his own country of Greece.[29]

After entering the practice of law in Rome, Cicero took part in several marquis trials (culminating in his victory in *In Verrem*), and was eventually, at his professional zenith, considered the greatest lawyer in the Republic.[30] He was first elected to public office at the age of thirty, and was eventually elected Consul at forty-two in 64 B.C.[31] During his Consulship, Cicero was responsible for thwarting the Cataline Conspiracy to overthrow the Senate, but in so doing he arguably violated several due process laws, including ordering the extrajudicial killings of several conspirators who had been Roman citizens, and whom critics argued should have received trials before being

---

[22] Marcus Tullius Cicero, *Political Speeches,* trans. D.H. Berry (New York, NY: Oxford University Press Inc., 2006) xii-xxx.
[23] *Id.*
[24] *Id.*
[25] "In Verres, Cicero", www.law2.umkc.edu/faculty/projects/ftrials/verres/verrescicero.html accessed November 8 2014.
[26] *Id.*
[27] See generally *id.*
[28] "In Verres, Cicero", www.law2.umkc.edu/faculty/projects/ftrials/verres/verrescicero.html accessed November 8 2014.
[29] *Id.*
[30] Marcus Tullius Cicero, *Political Speeches,* trans. D.H. Berry (New York, NY: Oxford University Press Inc., 2006) xii-xxx.
[31] *Id.*

executed. As a result of his actions to suppress the conspiracy, Cicero was eventually exiled (though he left of his own volition) following the conclusion of his term in office.[32] Shortly thereafter, the Tribunes of the Plebes caused a motion to pass in the Senate recalling Cicero to Rome. Upon his return, Cicero was greeted with approval and support by the people, and was reinstated to the Senate.[33] 'Then came the assassination of Caesar in 44 B.C…Cicero…at the age of 63…threw his energy into the struggle for the freedom of the republic. He became the life and soul of the senatorial party…[h]is last oratorical efforts were…hurled against Antony, in which he declared the tyrant to be a public enemy, and called upon the Romans to maintain their liberty. But the voice of her greatest orator could not save the state.'[34]

The Triumvirate that followed, and the subsequent Caesarian period, marked the end of the Republic, and are well known enough not to need recounting here. As a result of his opposition to Mark Antony specifically, and to the fall of the republic generally, Cicero was assassinated on December 7, 43 B.C.[35] It was towards the end of his life that Cicero wrote the majority of his treatises about jurisprudential theory. The culmination of his natural law theory would be found in his publication of *The Republic* and *The Laws*. These two books, merged into one publication, encapsulate the breadth of Cicero's natural law postulations.[36]

3. *IN VERREM*, THE CASE, THE TRIAL, AND THE OUTCOME

There is no clear indication as to why Cicero moved from practical considerations of lawyering and politicking to more esoteric postulations about the Natural Law. It may have been due to his desire to leave a legacy, or because he foresaw the end of the Republic due to the increasingly volatile political climate in Rome and wanted to preserve republican ideals for later generations in writing. In any case, it is apparent that Cicero dedicated the latter part of his life to *The Republic* and *The Laws*.

It is clear that Cicero would not likely have achieved such prominence in the Roman legal community, much less the Roman political realm, had he not shocked his contemporaries by way of his brilliant lawyering and oratory during the very public trial of the corrupt governor of Sicily, Verres. Had

[32] *Id.*

[33] *Id.*

[34] "In Verres, Cicero", www.law2.umkc.edu/faculty/projects/ftrials/verres/verrescicero.html accessed November 8 2014.

[35] *Id.*

[36] Marcus Tullius Cicero, *The Republic and The Laws,* trans. Niall Rudd (New York, NY: Oxford University Press Inc., 2008) x-xxxi.

Cicero not undertaken, and succeeded in, the prosecution of Verres, he might never have become leader of the pro-republican faction of the senate, he might never have been elected Consul, and therefore he would probably not have written *The Republic* and *The Laws* (and if he had, it is likely no one would have taken notice).

3.1. The Trial and Other Contemporaneous Happenings of Note

The trial known as *In Verrem* was revolutionary for its time (70 B.C.). Verres was a powerful and well-connected man and a high-born member of the aristocracy. He believed himself to be beyond reproach.[37] When he was appointed to the governorship of the Roman province of Sicily, he executed a systematic campaign of thievery, extra-judicial killings of both Romans and non-Romans alike, coercion, piracy, and great sexual depravity, including the raping the wives of prominent Sicilian citizens.[38] While the people of Sicily themselves were not Roman citizens at the time, they were viewed as citizens of a Roman protectorate, and therefore they were of import to the Roman world-view.[39] Furthermore, many of Verres' victims had been Roman citizens, principally merchants, who he falsely accused of piracy. When they could not, or did not, pay an extortion fee to Verres, he summarily declared their guilt and executed them, often in public.[40]

As all Roman citizens were entitled to due process under Roman law, these crimes were unfathomable to even the elite in Roman society. It was often boasted by many a Roman that if a man were to utter the phrase 'I am a Roman citizen' anywhere in the known world, he would be safe from persecution, let, or undue hindrance.[41]

Finally, the people of Sicily, desperate and otherwise without recourse, petitioned Rome for relief. They were ignored, likely due to the political dynamics of the day: it was commonly known that Verres' faction was about to take control of the Senate and that the incoming Consuls would be sympathetic to him, as well as rather merciless to his opponents.[42] Cicero however, a rather newly-minted lawyer and a junior member of the Senate, took it upon himself to investigate, and if necessary, defend the people of

---

[37] Marcus Tullius Cicero, *Political Speeches,* trans. D.H Berry (New York, NY: Oxford University Press Inc., 2006) xii-xxx.
[38] *Id.*
[39] *Id.*
[40] *Id.*
[41] *Id.*
[42] *Id.*

Sicily by bringing charges against Verres in the 'Roman Court of Corruption'.[43]

Throughout the course of his investigation, his witnesses and evidence were repeatedly destroyed or absconded by Verres' agents and those of his political allies in Rome. Several threats were made against Cicero's life leading up to the trial itself.[44] Nevertheless, Cicero, using his own funds, was able to craft a case against Verres. In a trial, where Cicero came up against the finest lawyer in Rome, Quintus Hortensius Hortelus, Cicero was able to persuade the jury of Verres' guilt.[45] In a series of what have been described as some of the best speeches ever delivered, Cicero thoroughly defeated Hortensius' case in defense of Verres. Pressured by the on-looking masses of Roman citizens (as all trials in Rome were open to the public), the Jury was ready to find Verres guilty on all counts.[46] Before a sentence could be handed down, which would have very likely entailed the seizure of all of Verres' property, and perhaps even his execution, Verres fled Rome with as much of his wealth as he and his entourage could manage to carry.[47]

By the end of the trial, which had been part of the public consciousness at the time, Cicero was widely considered to be the best lawyer in Rome, and his services were sought out by the rich and powerful among Rome's senate.[48] Due to the high profile nature of the trial, and the fact that it had been held in public, Cicero was, at the trial's conclusion, a household name in Rome.[49]

4. THE TRIAL'S IMPACT ON THE COURSE OF JURISPRUDENTIAL HISTORY

At this point in the discussion, it has been established that Cicero's victory in *In Verrem* greatly affected his career. As a result of the trial's effect upon Cicero's career, it was also of significant impact upon the trajectory of Roman politics. Nevertheless, in order to adequately demonstrate that these things affected the evolution of Natural Law Theory in the way that this paper's thesis argues them to have done, this discussion necessarily turns towards the defining (though by no means exhaustive defining) of the Natural Law Theory as well as the delineation of a substantial causal and chronological nexus between Natural Law Theory, particularly in its more contemporary forms, and the postulations of Cicero in his time.

---

[43] *Id.*
[44] *Id.*
[45] *Id.*
[46] *Id.*
[47] *Id.*
[48] *Id.*
[49] *Id.*

4.1. Cicero's Impact Upon the Trajectory of Natural Law Theory

Kevin Ryan, when expounding upon his view that the foundation of the United States of America as a modern republic was substantially related to the natural law views held by its founders, wrote, '[t]he settlers of America believed that identifiable moral, legal, and political principles were written in the nature of things, where they were discoverable by the free exercise of the mind; they believed that it is within the native powers of the human intellect, especially when disciplined by logic and careful reflection on experience, to discover the highest metaphysical truths.'50 Ryan goes on to discuss the distinction between the post-medieval view of natural rights and the pre-medieval view of natural law, and, noting their focuses to be rather distinct, he states that '[t]he philosophy of natural rights grew out of the works of seventeenth century continental writers, such as Grotius, Pufendorf, and Burlamaqui, as well as the English lawyers, theorists, and controversialists of the same period, from Coke to Milton, Sidney, and Locke.'[51] The Lockean view of Natural Law, which was fundamental in the formation of the United States of America as a modern republic, is one which portrays people as possessing of inalienable (universal) rights which prevail upon all, in all places at all times, because, before people are citizens, they are human beings.[52] Considering that many of the founders of the United States were ideologically informed by natural law thinkers such as John Locke, that the Constitution of the United States is laden with natural law references, and that the American Republican political model bears significant resemblance to that of the Roman Republic, it can be rationally inferred that the similarities between the Roman Republic and the United States of America are more than merely superficial. Additionally, if Natural Law Theory, as Ryan suggests, evolved from a discussion of the nature of law to one of individual rights, then it is apparent that, for such an evolution to have taken place, the theory not only predates its modern incarnation, but has causally resulted in its very existence today. After all, if, as the modern Natural Law Theory provides, there are natural rights held by all, surely there must be a reason for those rights to be considered natural and universal.

In his in discussion of Professor Lon Fuller's brand of Natural Law Theory, Douglas Strum describes natural law 'as meaning an oughtness or normativeness that in some sense is objective (that is, real, independent of any acknowledgement of its reality) and that to some extent can be discovered by

---

[50] Kevin F. Ryan, Esq., "We Hold These Truths" [Winter 2005-2006] Vt. B.J., at 9, 11.

[51] *Ibid.,* citing Benjamin Fletcher Wright, Jr., *American Interpretations of Natural Law: A Study in the History of Political Thought* (Cambridge Mass: Harvard University Press, 1931).

[52] *Id.*

means of man's powers of apprehension'.[53] Louis Hensler III's discussion of the origins of natural law centers upon Thomas Aquinas, whom he believes to be the originator of modern natural law theory. After discussing a post-modern renaissance of the aforesaid as outlined by Budziszewski in his own writings, Hensler states that '[n]either Budziszewski nor Lord Coke's understanding of the natural law is entirely original; they inherited this view of the natural law from the most influential natural law theorist of all time, the thirteenth-century Dominican monk, St. Thomas Aquinas.'[54] While this discussion carries the historical line further back than docs Douglas Strum (who ends his historical journey at Thomas Aquinas), it nevertheless lends credence to the notion that the modern natural law tradition cannot be said to exist in a temporal void; it is clear that it did not simply spring into existence at the time of John Locke or the American founders.

Pondering the renaissance of the Natural Law Theory, Kirk Kennedy theorizes that there are several types of natural law. He describes Classical natural law (embodied by Cicero), modern natural law (demonstrated by the Hart-Fuller debate), and post-modern natural law theories (as postulated by John Finnis among others).[55] 'Classical natural law is a prescriptive system that recognizes the existence of laws and rights antecedent to the creation of the state. These immutable laws and rights can be discovered by resort to human reason and by examining the fundamental nature of man and his environment...[n]atural law...while not a peculiarly Christian invention, traces its origins to the great thinkers and scholars of Western Civilization. . . .'[56]

It seems therefore, that the consensus among post-modern deliberants of the Natural Law Theory is that while the natural law finds its origins in Antiquity, it has grown and evolved through a series of historical phases, through which its focus has shifted from the original Ciceran or Greek view (which focused mainly upon the universal natural of law as preceding the state and its laws) to the modern and post-modern bents which prefer to view the natural law through an individualist lens which focuses more heavily on inalienable individual rights. The scholarly discussions referenced above do not by any means exhaust the field of discussion on the Natural Law Theory, but they clearly ponder the trajectory and evolution of the natural law as a theory by dissecting its various defenders' takes on the meaning of natural law. Having demonstrated that Natural Law theory is a product of ancient

---

[53] Douglas Sturm, "Lon Fuller's Multidimensional Natural Law Theory" [1966] 18 Stan. L. Rev. 612, 613.
[54] Louis W. Hensler III, "A Modest Reading of St. Thomas Aquinas on the Connection Between Natural Law and Human Law" [2009] 43 Creighton L. Rev. 153.
[55] Kirk A. Kennedy, "Reaffirming the Natural Law Jurisprudence of Justice Clarence Thomas" [1997] 9 Regent U. L. Rev. 33, 41.
[56] *Id.*

history, and that it does not stand alone in a temporal void as a product of postmodern thought alone, all that remains is to demonstrate the Cicero, at one time the most influential jurist in Rome, actually caused the aforesaid trajectory to occur.

Cicero's two late-in-life promulgated tomes, *The Republic* and *The Laws* were the culmination of his life's work. In them, Cicero discusses at length what would later become known as natural law. Natural law is the foundation for his view of what law ought to be. Throughout both books, he explains at length what the ideal legal and political system should resemble, and he justifies his statements with several key monologues. Here a few choice quotes will be extracted from those monologues to demonstrate the fact that his postulations are clearly the first embodiment of a Natural Law Theory.

As stated before, while several of the Greek thinkers of Antiquity espoused one or another principle mirrored in Cicero's work (which he himself admits in the aforementioned tomes), *The Republic* and *The Laws* are chronologically the first to treat the nature of law in a systemic fashion, having been written towards the end of Cicero's life almost twenty-one centuries ago.[57] Throughout *The Republic* and *The Laws,* Cicero seeks not only to expound upon what the ideal republican political and legal system should resemble, but perhaps more importantly, he endeavors to explain why it should do so. When expounding upon the nature of law as being more than simply a set of dictates from an emperor, Cicero states that 'law is the highest reason, inherent in nature, which enjoins what ought to be done and forbids the opposite'.[58] He later goes on to explain that 'law is a force of nature, the intelligence and reason of a wise man, and the criterion of justice and injustice'.[59] Within the same vein of thought, Cicero provides that '[t]here is one, single, justice. It binds together human society, and has been established by one, single, law. That law is right reason in commanding or forbidding'.[60] Summarizing the nature of law, he declares that 'law was not thought up by human beings, nor is it some kind of resolution passed by communities, but an external force that rules the world by its prohibitions and commands.'[61] Foreshadowing a phrase which would come to appear regularly in his rhetoric (right reason), Cicero postulates that 'there is but one essential justice which cements society, and one law which establishes justice. This law is right reason, which is the true rule of all commandments and prohibitions'.[62]

---

[57] Marcus Tullius Cicero, *The Republic and The Laws,* trans. Niall Rudd (New York, NY: Oxford University Press Inc., 2008) x-xxxi.

[58] *Id.* at 103.

[59] *Id.*

[60] *Id.* at 112.

[61] *Id.* at 124.

[62] Marcus Tullius Cicero, *On The Nature of The Gods, Divination, Fate, The Republic, Laws Et Cetera,* trans. C.D. Yonge (London, England: George Bell and Sons 1878) 417.

Near the end of his writings in favour of *The Republic*, while being tacitly critical of the Civil Law, Cicero explains why laws must be understood to be more than mere imperial dictates crafted at the whims of sovereigns. He provides that, 'law in the proper sense is right reason in harmony with nature. It is spread throughout the whole human community, unchanging and eternal…[t]his law cannot be countermanded, nor can it be totally rescinded…[t]here will not be one such law in Rome and another in Athens…but all peoples at all times will be embraced by a single and eternal unchangeable law'.[63] When viewing all of the above in context, Cicero's main postulations seem to coalesce around the notion that true law is universal in its origin and its application throughout all times and in all places, it is unalterable, and it can be discovered only by use of right reason and not by way of imperial dictates. Both chronology and the content of Cicero's *The Republic* and *The Laws,* when contrasted to the content of the works of Aquinas, Locke, Fuller, *et al.,* demonstrate that his treatise was the first to craft a Natural Law Theory. As to the distinction between the Natural Law Theory of Antiquity, and its post-modern incarnation, the former focuses more on the universal nature of law, while the latter focuses heavily on natural (inalienable) rights. The later can only exist as a consequence of the former; for any right to be natural (inalienable), it must originate from a law transcending all temporal normative orders (such as imperial law, or more recently, positivist law). In other words, natural rights derive their moral, philosophical, or legal *raison d'être* directly from the existence of natural law. Therefore, while Cicero may not have focused on individual natural rights, he outlined that natural law was the basis for all just, universally applicable, and immutable law. One need not delve too far below the surface to see that individual natural rights are simply the result of natural law when viewed from the perspective of the individual.

5. CONCLUSION

In sum, it is evident that not only was Cicero's Natural Law Theory the first in time, but it is also clear that all modern and post-modern takes on the natural law rely on the assumption that his basic premise is true: without a universal immutable law that applies to all people, in all times and places, there can be no notion of natural or inalienable rights. It is ultimately impossible to know if a man of such great quality as that possessed by Cicero would have risen to prominence by way of some other accomplishment, had he lost the trial known as *In Verrem*. We do know, however, that it was his victory over

[63] Marcus Tullius Cicero, *The Republic and The Laws,* trans. Niall Rudd (New York, NY: Oxford University Press Inc., 2008) 68-69.

Hortensius in that trial that *did* directly result in his professional and political success. If Cicero had not become the foremost lawyer in Rome, had not become the leader of the pro-republican faction within the Senate, and had not been elected Consul, even if he had still written *The Republic* and *The Laws*, who would have read it?

The Intricacies of Partly New Inventions: Should We Grant Patentability?

Anatoli Tsakalidou[1]

This article addresses the issue of partly new inventions and the possibility of granting them patentability. The route of the analysis starts with the identification of the sectors in which this issue frequently arises. It consequently continues with finding and locating all those common characteristics of the circumstances under which the 'phenomenon'-in-question arises. The interesting conclusion of this analysis is that the phenomenon of partially new inventions being granted patentability occurs mainly within the pharmaceutical (and chemicals) sector. This realization leads to even more substantial concerns, especially from a competition law perspective. That is because pharmaceutical (and chemicals) companies apply for – and get granted- patentability of partly new inventions to a wide extent. One of the questions at this point is whether this is causing a restriction to competition by threatening the delicate balances of the specific market. This question is answered through references not only to the law itself, including leading case-law from both the EU and the UK, but also to policy concerns and market-related considerations. Finally, the aforementioned findings are used in order to address the question of whether patentability should be granted to partly new inventions, whilst following a further analysis and assessment of relevant competition -and other- policy issues.

Keywords: patents, European Union, EPC 1973, EPC 2000, pharmaceuticals, competition law.

[1] LLM, International Commercial Law, University of Nottingham.

1. Introduction

Patentability is granted where the claimed invention fulfills the requirements of novelty, inventiveness and industrial application[2]. That means that the invention would have to be new[3]; that it is not obvious to the person skilled in the art[4]; and that it can have a use in industry[5]. What about the case, though, when a claimed invention is not entirely new? Can it be granted patentability? And if so, under which requirements? In the present essay we will look into the issue of patentability for partially new inventions. In Chapter II we will identify the problematic areas of partially new inventions; in chapter III we will present the issue of inventive step with regards to these inventions; and in chapter IV we will look into the policy rationale of granting patentability for partially new inventions by taking into consideration the particularities of the sectors from where these inventions are derived.

2. Novelty

When an invention is 'new' in its totality, then there is no problem; it can be declared new, thus fulfilling the novelty requirement and passing the first 'test' of patentability. Problems, however, arise in circumstances where some parts are new and some are not; thus novelty, we could say, is marginal[6]. In the present chapter, we will examine the instances where an invention is considered new in part. In that regard, we will look into the specific categories of inventions that have caused the most problems and subsequent critique: we will first examine the case of exceptions to the medical/pharmaceutical field, then the exception to non-medical uses and finally, we will examine the issue of selection patents.

2.1. An exception to an exception: The case of medicine and pharmaceuticals

Article 52(1) of the 1973 EPC stated in substance that patentability could be recognized in inventions which are novel, inventive and industrially applicable, so that new uses for known products can be protected as such by

---

[2] Paul Torremans, *Holyoak and Torremans: Intellectual Property Law*, Seventh Edition, Oxford University Press, 2013, Chapter 4.
[3] UK Patent Act 1977, s. 1 (1) (a).
[4] UK Patent Act 1977 s. 3.
[5] UK Patent Act 1977 s. 4 (1).
[6] Charlotte Waelde, Graeme Laurie, Abbe Brown, Smita Kheria, Jane Cornwell, *Contemporary Intellectual Property*, Third Edition, Oxford University Press, 2014, 439.

claims directed to that use. That was valid for all fields but one: the field of making products for use in surgery, therapy and diagnostic methods. However, an exception laid in 54(5) EPC 1973 (and the relevant s. 2(6) of the 1977 Act), namely that so far as the first use of medicaments is concerned, the required novelty for the medicament, which forms the subject-matter of the claim, is derived from the new pharmaceutical use. Than meant that if a known drug would be used for a new treatment, then novelty could be claimed. The limitation inherent therein was that the known substance should not have been known to have any medicinal use before. However, soon enough, practice showed that novelty could be claimed not only for the first medical use, but also for any –second- subsequent use. That was the conclusion of the Eisai/Second Medical Indication Case[7] on the European Level and the John Wyeth[8] case in the UK. Both cases concluded that art. 54 (5) of the EPC and s. 2 (6) of the Act also applied to second medical uses, rather than just first ones, under the requirement that claims for second medical use were introduced in the form of 'Swiss-type claims': 'use of substance X for the manufacture of a medicament for the treatment of Y'. That was the case, because, if the form 'use of substance X for the treatment of Y' was used, then such claims would fall under the exception of 'methods of treatment'[9], whereas Swiss type claims were focused on the manufacture of the medicament by using the known substance in question, thus deriving their novelty from the new therapeutic use[10] (purpose). After the first cases, others followed[11]. So it became clear that when an old drug was used for the treatment of a different disease, novelty could be granted.

What about the case though, when the known drug would treat the same disease but the alleged novel part was that of the method of administration or dosage? The opinions on the European and UK level differ; EPC 1973 in its application by the EBoA came to cover patentability of substances and compositions known in the prior art for use in the treatment by therapy of a particular disease, even if they were directed to the treatment of the same illness, provided this treatment was new and inventive; that was enshrined in rigorous case law[12]. Hence, new use could either mean that a disease could be now treated by the claimed substance/composition, or that it included different steps applicable (by their nature) to a therapeutic method which may not be

[7] Eisai, G5/83 [1985] OJ EPO 64.
[8] *John Wyeth & Brother Ltd's Application* [1985] RPC 545.
[9] Article 52 (4) of the EPC and s 4 (2) of the Act.
[10] Horton, 'Methods of Treatment and Second Medical Use', Patent World 9, 2000.
[11] See (G-1/83) Bayer and (G-7/83) Pharmuka, Decision of the Enlarged Board of Appeal dated December 5, 1984 [1985] OJ EPO 60.
[12] T 19/86, OJ EPO 1989, 24, T 893/90 of 22 July 1993, T 233/96 of 4 May 2000, 51/93 of 8 June 1994, T 138/95 of 12 October 1999, T 290/86, OJ EPO 1992, 414, T 254/93, OJ EPO 1998, 285 and in the UK, see *Actavis UK v Merck* [2008] EWCA Civ 444 (CA).

claimed as such. In the UK, there had been doubts[13], until they eventually permitted the aforementioned practice[14], thus following the decisions of Eisai and Genentech[15].

As is probably assumed, the use of Swiss-type claims brought much criticism, due to the problematic 'functional relationship of the features (belonging to therapy) conferring novelty and inventiveness, if any, and the claimed manufacturing process'[16].

After the 2000 revision of the EPC, and while EPC 1973 (decision Eisai G 5/83) allowed claims directed to the use of a substance for the manufacture of the drug for a therapeutic indication ("Swiss-type claims")[17], art. 54 (5) now explicitly permits the use of purpose-related product claims, directed to the substance itself[18]. Following that, the UK also implemented that development in art 4A (4) of the Act. So, now, purpose-related product protection can be officially granted for second medical uses[19]. How should these be claimed now, though?

As noted in the Dosage regime/ABBOTT RESPIRATORY[20] case, "It appears that the rights conferred on the patentee by the claim category under Art. 54(5) EPC are likely broader, and could, in particular, lead to possible restrictions on the freedom of medical practitioners to prescribe or administer generics.[21]" That being said, the Board, concluded that, patent applications filed from 29 January 2011 and with no earlier priority date will not be granted European patents under Swiss-type use claims[22], where the subject

---

[13] *Bristol Meyers Squibb Co v Baker Norton Pharmaceuticals* [2001] RPC 1; *American Home Products Coo v Novartis Pharmaceuticals UK Ltd* [2001] RPC 159

[14] *Actavis UK Ltd v Merck & Co Inc* [2008] EWCA Civ 444; [2008] RPC 26.

[15] See case commentary on *Actavis*, Paul England, Clare McDonald, 'Patents - the Court of Appeal upholds a patent for a new dosage regime', E.I.P.R. 2008, 30(9), N68-71 and *Genentech Case* [1989] RPC 613.

[16] http://www.epo.org/law-practice/case-law-appeals/recent/g080002ex1.html, section 7.1.3.

[17] Julian Cockbain, Sigrid Sterckx, 'Is the Enlarged Board of Appeal of the European Patent Office authorised to extend the bounds of the patentable? The G5/83 Second Medical Indication/EISAI and G2/08 Dosage Regime/ABBOTT RESPIRATORY cases', IIC 2011, 42(3), 257-271 at 262.

[18] The new Article 54(5) EPC eliminates any legal uncertainty on the patentability of further medical uses. It unambiguously permits purpose-related product protection for each further new medical use of a substance or composition already known as a medicine', explanatory notes MR/18/00, point 4.

[19] Lionel Bently, *Intellectual Property Law*, Third Edition, Oxford University Press, , 2009, p 481.

[20] G-2/08 Dosage regime/ABBOTT RESPIRATORY, 2010 OJ EPO 456-494. See 42 IIC 215 (2011).

[21] G-2/08 Dosage regime/ABBOTT RESPIRATORY, 2010 OJ EPO 456-494. See 42 IIC 215 (2011),at 490.

[22] Julian Cockbain, Sigrid Sterckx, 'Is the Enlarged Board of Appeal of the European Patent Office authorised to extend the bounds of the patentable? The G5/83 Second Medical

matter of a claim was rendered novel only by a new therapeutic use of a medicament (for example, a new dosage). Even though that does not exclude the possibility of granting patents where, for example, a dosage regime is the only novel feature claimed, it subsequently creates a blurry veil of uncertainty on cases which were granted patentability where the only novel element was for example, dosage regimes, under Swiss-type claims[23].

2.2. Non- Medical Use

The novelty of purpose applied in the medical field was applied in a non-medical field in the Mobil/Friction Reducing Additive case[24]. The patent in question related to the use of a known compound for use as an additive for lubricant oils. An earlier patent had been granted for the same additive and the same use. What the patentees claimed here as novel, was the purpose, namely, the purpose of reducing friction between sliding surfaces in an engine. The formulation of the problem here was the following: old substance, old use, new purpose: could this be considered novel? The EBoA, in this highly contentious case, concluded to the affirmative.

This case was in essence, a matter of second non-medical use, following the Eisai Case[25], even though the Board made sure to distinguish between the differences it found in these two cases[26]. In brief, the Court stated that this new use claimed by the patentees ought to have a technical effect accompanying the use, thus resulting in a technical feature that becomes part of the subject-matter of the use claim[27]. In this way, novelty will be declared, as long as this technical effect had not been 'made available to the public' through its previous use, despite the fact that this technical effect might have *taken place* during the previous use[28]. This last part reflected the shift of the English law regarding the lack of novelty in an invention which had previous secret use[29], in the sense that that secret use anticipated the later invention. Furthermore, in Robertet/Deodorant compositions[30] it was submitted that the patentee has to

---

Indication/EISAI and G2/08 Dosage Regime/ABBOTT RESPIRATORY cases', IIC 2011, 42(3), 257-271 at 258.

[23] See for example *Actavis UK v Merck* [2008] EWCA Civ 444 (CA).

[24] G2/88 [1990] EPOR 73.

[25] Eisai Case, *supra* note 6.

[26] Gerald Paterson, 'The novelty of Use Claims', IIC 1996, 27(2), 179-190, at 184.

[27] In the sense that, as Bently states, achieving the new purpose is seen as a 'technical feature' of the invention, Lionel Bently, *supra*, 483.

[28] *Supra* at 10.3

[29] See *Bristol Myer's Application* [1975] RPC 127, which was under the Patent Act 1949.

[30] T892/94 [1999] EPOR 516, 526, where novelty of purpose was not granted for the effect of the aromatic esters on the human skin, based on the argument that claimed effect was nothing more than a disclosure of already existing information.

submit a new purpose and that disclosure of already existing information would not grant novelty[31]. This meant that novelty could be recognised with regards to 'technical effects' under the aforementioned requirements.

The Mobil case represents good law in the UK that not only relates to chemical compounds, but also to other non-medical areas that strive to discover new applications of already known compounds[32]. However, one should underline the legitimate concerns that followed it. *First,* as Aplin[33] notes, following the opinion of Lord Hoffmann in Merrell Dow v Norton[34], allowing such novelty of purpose claims can have significant negative impact on deciding patent infringement, since there is no way of knowing whether using the known substance is done with the old or new purpose in mind, thus creating an uncertain ground for infringement. The *second* problem derives from a competition law perspective: the Mobil case had the important negative effect of allowing re-monopolisation of the same substance that had been monopolised through the first patent[35].

2.3. Selection Patents

The third main area where an invention could be considered partially new is the area of selection patents, mainly referring to –but not exclusively confined to- chemicals[36] . When a scientist is doing research, he/she makes different combinations of compounds, which result in broad classes of chemicals, the specific uses or advantages of which have not been discovered usually. In general, this extensive monopoly –which not only distorts the market but also acts as a disincentive for further research- is balanced with selection patents, under which, even though a generic disclosure of the class of chemicals had occurred already, the second patentee may be granted a patent for a selection of substances from the general class as disclosed by the first research[37].

The problem inherent to selection patents is visible already from the description: can one really declare something novel if it had already been disclosed? Moreover, had that disclosure established anticipation? A first answer was given by the IG Farbenindustrie case[38], which set three conditions

---

[31] See also on this issue Catherine Colston and Jonathan Galloway, *Modern Intellectual Property Law*, 3d edition, Routledge, 2013, 183-184.
[32] As noted by Bently in Lionel Bently, *supra*, p 482.
[33] Tanya Aplin, Jennifer Davis, *Intellectual Property Law*, 2nd edition, Oxford University Press, 2013, 677.
[34] [1996] RPC 76, 92.
[35] Catherine Colston and Jonathan Galloway, *supra*, 183-184.
[36] Catherine Colston and Jonathan Galloway, *supra*, 180.
[37] The first case to consider selection patents in the UK was *IG Farbenindustrie* [1930] 47 RPC 289, 322-3.
[38] *IG Farbenindustrie* [1930] 47 RPC 289.

for a selection patent to be valid[39]: first, that the selection was based on substantial advantage resulting from the use of selected parts, second that all these selected parts demonstrated this advantage and third, that in the case certain quality was the basis of the selection, then this quality should be also unique[40] to the selected members of the group[41]. Selection patents thus, are founded on 'new uses'[42], although not limited to them[43]. Even though the patent in this case was not held to be valid after all, numerous cases that followed it[44], relied on it and explored further the notion of selection patents, usually resulting in the validation of selection patents.

The situation has now changed after Dr. Reddy's Laboratories Ltd v Eli and Co Ltd[45], mostly with regard to the aforementioned conditions set as rules to decide on patentability. Jacob LJ mentioned[46] that IG Farbenindustrie should not be followed, since, first, it was under the old law of 1949 which did not identify between novelty and inventive step (in fact, the conditions themselves in this case portray this confusion), second, the EPO had never used these or any equivalent conditions or rules with regards to selection patents; and finally, third, it made things difficult for the patentee, since he/she would have to engage in multiple and (maybe unrealistically) extensive experimentation in order to prove that the selected class had a substantial advantage[47]. Instead, the Court decided to follow the EPO Board's approach, which is more novelty- and non-obviousness-oriented. In this way, selection patents will not be treated as an exception to the novelty rules. It should be pointed out at this point that EPO's case law treats selection patents under the general novelty requirements[48]. This means[49] that the previous disclosure of

[39] Note however that Torremans, Holyoak and Torremans, *supra,* 70; see also Lionel Bently, *supra* 2009, 485, who places these requirements under novelty, whereas Winfried Tilmann sets them under inventive step; see Winfried Tilmann, 'Validity of selective product claims', Venice Conferences III and V, Lundbeck and Olanzapin, IIC 2010, 41(2), 149-169, at 160.

[40] On this point see also *Shell Refining Marketing & Marketing Co Ltd* [1960] RPC 35 at 55.

[41] See further Lionel Bently, *supra*, 485, Aplin, *supra*, 679-680, Colston, *supra*, 181.

[42] Colston, *supra*, 181.

[43] Lionel Bently, *supra*, 486 where he states that they can also apply to the discovery of new substances, new uses for old substances or even new purposes for old substances processed in old ways.

[44] See especially the last case under the previous law: *El Du Pont de Nemours & Co's (Witsiepe's) Application* [1982] FSR 303; *Boehringer Mannheim v Genzyme* [1993] FSR 716; *Beechan Group Ltd v Bristol Laboratories International SA* [1978] RPC 521.

[45] *Dr Reddy's Laboratories (UK) Ltd v Eli and Co Ltd* [2009] EWCA 1362; [2010] RPC 9.

[46] *Ibid.* at 35-37.

[47] *Ibid.* at 39.

[48] See for example Sanofi/Enantiomer, T658/91 [1996] EPOR 24 or Bayer/Diastereomers, T12/81 OJ EPO 296; [1979-85] EPOR B-308.

[49] More on enabling disclosure, see *General Tire & Rubber Co. v Firestone Tyre & Rubber Co* [1972] RPC 457; *Asaho Kasei Kogyo's KK's Application* [1991] RPC 485; *Biogen Inc v Medeva plc* [1997] RPC 1.

the class will have to be enabling[50], in the sense that the disclosure allows the skilled person to work on the invention[51].

3. INVENTIVE STEP

The next condition that needs to be fulfilled so that an invention is patentable, is s. 3 of the Act[52]. According to this condition, unless the invention is obvious to a person skilled in the art, 'having regard to any matter which forms part of the state of the art', it will involve an inventive step; hence it will fulfil the condition spelled out in s. 3 of the Act. It ensures a qualitative assessment of the patent which results in patenting meritorious[53] inventions instead of obvious ones, which would imply only repeating or slightly modifying prior art[54].

3.1. Assessing the problems of inventiveness

The case law on the patentability requirement of inventive step has been extensive. Besides the guidance it has provided us with, it has revealed many problematic areas in situations when only 'partial novelty' exists, thus rendering the clarity of the inventive step requirement harder. These problems will be discussed in this sub-chapter.

3.1.1. Partial Novelty in the Medical/ Pharmaceutical/ Chemistry Sector

It is now widely known that the Windsurfing case[55] introduced an inventiveness test comprising four gradual questions[56]in order to decide

---

[50] See *Synthon BV v Smithkline Beecham plc* [2005] AII ER (D), 235, [2006] RPC 10 (HL), where the test applied was not enabling disclosure, but two different elements: disclosure and enablement.

[51] See Bently, *supra*, 486-487.

[52] And subsequent article 56 of the EPC.

[53] Tanya Aplin, Jennifer Davis, *supra*, 685.

[54] A. Griffiths, 'Windsurfing and the Inventive Step' [1999] IPQ 160, 163-164.

[55] *Windsurfing International Inc v Tabur Marine (Great Britain) Ltd* [1985] RPC 59.

[56] The questions are: (1) identify the inventive concept embodied in the patent in suit; (2) assume the mantle of the normally skilled but unimaginative addressee in the art at the priority date and impute to him what was, at that date, common general knowledge in the art in question; (3) identify what, if any, differences exist between the matter cited as being [state of the art] and the alleged invention; (4) ask whether, viewed without any knowledge of the alleged invention, those differences constitute steps which would have been obvious to the skilled man or whether they require a degree of invention *Windsurfing International Inc v Tabur Marine (Great Britain) Ltd* [1985] R.P.C. 59 at 73-74.

whether something is obvious or not. That test was later on modified when the Court of Appeal was considering the Pozzoli case[57] (Pozzoli test). So, now the first question of the test regards the 'normally skilled but unimaginative addressee in the art' and the common general knowledge in the art-in question that can be attributed to him/her. The test itself had raised many questions relating to its effect, until it was held in the Conor case[58] that the test was to be seen as a guideline and not as a route to a definitive answer.

Further –and more intense- questions[59] had been raised regarding the addressee of the test. The Pfizer case[60] showed that this person is just a creation made up to serve the purposes of the test and that it did not correspond to a real person. It was also held in the same case that this creation, this person, has relevant knowledge of the particular field discussed pertaining to the patent. Is that person the same in any case?

Genentech[61] concluded that it isn't. In particular, it stated that due to the highly intellectual area (biotech), the hypothetical addressee should raise the bar high[62]; because of the nature of the field, where invention is a primary goal that characterises to a wide extent the industry, the 'person skilled in the art' should also have inventive capacity. That can have significant repercussions on relevant fields, such as the ones where partially-new 'inventions' –in the broad sense- exist, namely medicine, pharmaceuticals and chemicals. In these areas, most of the researchers have obtained high education, including usually a PhD or equivalent[63]. The result of that would be that in all the relevant fields, such as the ones we are discussing, solutions (or developments) that are considered as an inventive step, are classified as obvious[64], going against the letter of s. 3 of the Act.

Another view expressed in the same case that could prove problematic for the particular fields under review now, is the view expressed by Mustill LJ[65] that the time and money spent on the particular research do not suffice and that the law as it is, needs something additional. Even though it appears to be a fairly legitimate aspect, it should be noted that especially in the fields-in-question, time and money spent on any research can reach to significant amounts, not to mention that, as Purchas LJ[66] suggested, to the contrary,

---

[57] *Pozzoli SPA v BDMD SA* [2007] FSR 37 (CA).
[58] *Conor Medsystems Inc v Angiotech Inc* [2007] ECWA Civ 5.
[59] See further Holyoak and Torremans, *supra*, 76-79.
[60] *Pfizer Ltd Patent* [2001] FRS (16).
[61] *Genentech Inc Patent* [1989] RPC 147.
[62] *ibid.*, at 214
[63] See Torremans, *supra*, 81-82.
[64] *Ibid.*, 89.
[65] Genentech, *supra*, 280.
[66] *Ibid.*, 221.

significant time and money expenditures may actually provide a good indication of the non-obviousness of the subject-matter.

Finally, another problem created with a focus on the partial novelty discussed in the previous chapter, is exactly this: that not everything is new. So how will be decided whether the step made forward is an inventive one? If one follows the same logic adopted in Genentech[67], then in most of the cases that we described above, most of the materials, are lying on the road and 'are available for the research worker to pick them up'. Furthermore, since inventiveness needs to be assessed at every research stage, then that would imply that the focus should concentrate on 'the process and the materials employed, rather on their use and consequences'[68], in contrast to what Dillon LJ submitted in Genentech[69]. If that's the case, then proving that a 'clear inventive step' occurred might become significantly burdensome for firms of the sectors-in-questions whose alleged step forward might be 'merely' one novel aspect (use or purpose)[70].

3.1.2. Selection Patents

When it comes to selection patents, the first problem identified is one of clarity between the novelty and inventive step requirement. As noted before[71], opinions differ, which could also have to do with the inconsistencies sometimes noted on the European level[72]. Besides that, another problem that might arise in this instance is relatively obvious: since the broader class the selected members belonged to was known, how will obviousness be assessed? The researcher will have to act in a technically creative fashion when doing the selection, thus a technical contribution is required based on some kind of logic, instead of arbitrariness (which is not deemed inventive in any field[73]). Furthermore, what is needed is that the technical aspect, on which the selection will be based on, could presumably characterise all the members of the selected group[74]. This could raise some questions as to the realism of the

---

[67] *Ibid.*, 243.

[68] See Torremans, *supra*, 86.

[69] '...empirical research industriously pursued may lead to a patentable invention', Genentech, *supra*, 241.

[70] See on this one also *Williams v Nye* [1980] 7 RPC 62; it was a case of mosaicking, where the combination of two similar machines operating related functions in order to establish a new use, was found lacking inventiveness.

[71] See section of novelty on selection patents .

[72] For example, Pfizer/Penem, T1042/92 [1995] EPOR 207 and Sanofi/Enantiomer, T658/91 [1996] EPOR 24.

[73] *Sandvik Intellectual Property AB v Kennametal UK Ltd* [2011] EWHC 3311, 185.

[74] *Dr. Reddy's Laboratories (UK) Ltd v Eli Lilly & Co Ltd* [2009] EWCA Civ 1362, [2010] RPC 9.

requirement, as well as to the requirement of 'fair assumption'[75], since both promote uncertainty with regards to the assessment of the existence of inventive step.

3.2. Assessing the Evidence of Inventiveness- The case of Secondary Evidence

In order to make its decision, the Court, may rely on secondary evidence, which have the function of providing support for the claim of non-obviousness. For the purposes of this essay, we shall examine the case of commercial success, which is inextricably connected with the long-felt want argument.

3.2.1. Long-felt-want

The implications of this argument are quite clear; it essentially bears the logic that the solution proposed by the claimant/patentee is non-obvious, because if it had been obvious, then it would have been invented earlier so that this long-felt-want of the people and the society could have been satisfied. Even though long-felt-want can be claimed at any time, its evaluation must be careful[76]. That is because it is merely an indication as to why the solution had not been given by someone else at an earlier stage. In that regard, case-law has structured some elements, functioning in a merely indicative way, such as the length of time that the particular need has been known or the extent to which materials and subsequent information used as the premises of the proposed solution had been available[77].

3.2.2. Commercial Success

Commercial success has been used as an argument to support non-obviousness on the basis that it fulfils a long-felt-want and because of this the proposed novel solution will enjoy commercial success, which consequently means that there was an inventive step when constructing the novel solution that the public warmly welcomed[78]. There are three main reasons why an argument of this kind is hard to work: first, commercial success is nowadays especially, a matter of advertising and distribution. Especially in the

---

[75] See Torremans *supra*, 87.
[76] Lionel Bently, *supra*, 505.
[77] Mentioned in Adolf Schindling/Illuminating device, T324/94 [1997] EPOR 146.
[78] Samuel Parkes & Co v Cocker Brothers Ltd [1929] 46 RPC 241, 248.

pharmaceutical and medical sector, where there is very effective distribution behind[79], it becomes more visible that acclamation by the public does not come on its own. Second, the test of obviousness bears a question of a technical nature, not a commercial[80]. Third, let us not forget that commercial success can only be evaluated as secondary evidence; therefore it has no further significance besides that[81].

3.3. Assessing the Patentability Requirements for partially-new inventions

After discussing all relevant aspects of the subject under examination, we need to go 'back to basics' in this chapter in order to explain the rationale of the patent system and the reasons why if something is new *in part* but involves a clear inventive step and fulfills a long-felt need is not necessarily patentable. It was explained in Chapter II that, when something is partially new, it does not follow that it will be necessarily considered novel in its entirety. And that is fair. The justification for that will be revealed in the sequence of the following thoughts:

Patents create monopolies, so, even by definition they create market distortions[82]. In that sense, one should be careful when interpreting the rules granting patentability so as to keep market distortions at the minimum possible level without, of course, limiting the scope of patent law in a disproportionate way.

The sectors that have raised most issues regarding products/processes that are partially new are two and they sometimes coincide: pharmaceutical/medical and chemical. Especially with regards to the first one, some definitions are in place. In order to understand the implications of partially new patents in the pharmaceutical sector, one would have to make reference as to how the pharmaceutical sector works. For our purposes, we need to identify between two main groups of pharmaceutical companies: originators or innovators and generics[83]. The first ones are those who invest funds in R&D and apply for drug patents. As for the second ones, they come into play after the patents of the originators have expired; they manufacture

---

[79] As noted in Barry Bleidt, "Recent Issues and Concerns about Pharmaceutical Industry Promotional Efforts" (1992) 22(2) Journal of Drug Issues 413, in many cases marketing costs exceed even R&D costs in the pharmaceutical industry.

[80] *Moelnlycke AB v Procter & Gamble Ltd (No. 3)* [1990] RPC 498, 503, as seen in Torremans, *supra*, 85.

[81] *Beloit Technologies Inc v Valmet Paper Machinery Inc* [1995] RPC 705.

[82] Jones Alison and Sufrin Brenda, *EU Competition Law*, 4th edition, Oxford University Press, 2011, 709-711.

[83] Paul England, 'Recent Developments in Pharmaceutical Secondary Patents in the light of the Commission's inquiry into the Pharmaceutical Sector', E.I.P.R. 2009 31(12), 614-622, 615.

the previously patented drugs and distribute them to the market at a fraction of the cost[84]. The Commission's recent Pharma investigation[85] was initiated due to competition concerns between these two groups. In specific, the Commission was concerned that originators engage in methods of patent evergreening[86] (by applying for second patents, selection patents and the like) that restrict market access to both generics and other originators, thus resulting in a negative overall impact on society and consumers, who would not be able to have access to cheaper generic drugs once the original patents expired[87]. Besides the obvious problem of remonopolising previous art (which is mostly the case with selection patents[88]), another, more important issue is created, considering the 'abusive' practices of evergreening that originators engage in. This problem is not merely restriction of competition per se, but the implications of this restriction on society[89]. In specific, if in any case partially new processes/products are capable of being granted patentability in the sectors in question (no matter if they involve a clear inventive step or not), then originator companies could have a free ticket to evergreening. That would consequently mean that generics would not be able to come into play and hence, prices for drugs would remain high to the detriment of consumers and in general, society. This is a big issue, especially considering the importance of health and accessibility to drugs[90].

---

[84] *Ibid.*

[85] European Commission, Competition DG, Pharmaceutical Sector Inquiry Final Report, 2009 http://ec.europa.eu/competition/sectors/pharmaceuticals/inquiry/staff_working_paper_part1.pdf.

[86] *Supra*, 615; When talking about generics, he states that they mostly want to evoke patents of innovators 'variously described as "secondary", "evergreening" or "life-cycle" patents. These patents do not protect the active ingredient that makes the drug effective as a treatment, but instead protect different physical forms of that drug, for example: different salts of the drug; dosage regimes; formulations; delivery devices and further medicinal uses'.

[87] In order to understand the significance of the issue better see Johnson & Johnson and Novartis Case where the Commission fined the two companies for infringement of art 101 TFEU because they agreed with a generics company in the Netherlands that the latter would abstain from bringing the patented drug for the treatment of cancer after their patent expired, see Press Release http://europa.eu/rapid/press-release_IP-13-1233_en.htm, found in EU Focus, Johnson & Johnson and Novartis fined for delaying market entry of pain-killer, EU Focus 2014, 316, 6.

[88] This is why, novelty should be, generally, given to those selections that entail restricted examples from the wider class which had not been tested or used before; in this way, no remonopolisation occurs, Catherine Colston and Jonathan Galloway, *supra* note 30, p 180-184

[89] For a thorough analysis see Steve D. Shadowen, Keith B. Leffler, Joseph T. Lukens, Bringing market discipline to pharmaceutical product reformulations, IIC 2011, 42(6), 698-725.

[90] See for example the impact of drug accessibility on HIV/Aids, Rachel Roumet, 'Access to patented anti-HIV/AIDS medicine: the South African experience', E.I.P.R. 2010, 32(3), 137-141.

On the other hand, especially because these industries play an important role as to whether and to what extent society will benefit, making patentability a very hard case (as it has become especially after the Genentech case in terms of inventive step), would create losses in the long-term. These losses will be borne by both the industries themselves –because they wouldn't get any fair returns on their previous investments resulting in discouragement of further research[91]- and the society- because if industries stop investing in research, then losses will be incurred in terms of possible benefits stemming from developments in the respective industries. That is in addition to the fact that "Patents are pivotal to the research-based pharmaceutical industry, given the enormous investment and risk required to develop innovative medicines. It can cost 1 billion or more to develop a new medicine in the period between discovery and marketing, normally a duration of 12 to 13 years. Only around 20% of new products ever recover the cost of development."[92] Furthermore, if patentability becomes very hard to prove, innovation will be impaired significantly, because it is the originators that both promote research and innovation via their patents and –usually- engaging in patent evergreening[93]; if they cannot have a fair access to patentability, then there will be nothing for the generics to provide to the market, as the latter do not engage in R&D[94]. From this aspect, there will be further losses.

Notwithstanding subsequent EU policy concerns that have to do mainly with the disadvantaged position of EU pharmaceuticals in comparison to American ones (and that would possibly constitute an incentive in order to grant patentability on less strict terms)[95], given the above, it is up to the courts to decide to what extent the anti-competitiveness of a patent is harmful and needs to be revoked (or not be granted in the first place, at least in the UK). In that way, a line between patentability and non-patentability will be drawn. In that regard, there is usually a fairly good reason why some 'inventions' (in the broad sense) in these sectors, when partially new, are not considered novel.

---

91 Amanda Odell-West, 'A proposal to amend the medical exclusion within patent law to provide for the patentability of certain methods of treatment', E.I.P.R. 2007, 29(12), 492-499.

92 EFPIA Factsheet: "Understanding patents and their vital role in medicine discovery", 1, http://www.efpia.eu/Content/Default.asp?PageID=559&DocID=5348 [Last Accessed May 12, 2014].

93 Carlos M. Correa, 'Efforts to raise the bar in patent examination need to be supported,' IIC 2012, 43(7), 747-750, who claims that the bar to patentability should be raised talks about relevant initiatives undertaken mainly in Brazil and Australia.

94 Nicoleta Tuominen, 'An IP perspective on defensive patenting strategies of the EU pharmaceutical industry', E.I.P.R. 2012, 34(8), 541-551.

95 The Directorate General for Enterprise and Industry of the European Commission suggests that the position of EU originators should be strengthened through the implementation of measures. Russell Graeme Hunter, *The Pharmaceutical Sector in the European Union, Intellectual Property Rights, Parallell Trade and Community Law*, Juristförlaget, Stockholm, 2001, 13.

The balance between competition concerns and patent rights of course, is not conducted only by the courts, but primarily by the law itself. Since this is the rationale of the law, it would be outside the scope of both competition law and patent law to assume that in any case that something is new in part as long as it fulfills a long-felt-want and the inventive step is clear, patentability can be granted.

4. CONCLUSIONS

It has become by now obvious that the question of whether partially new solutions/products/processes can be granted patentability is a difficult one. It is not merely a matter of strict provisions that are applied automatically regardless of the case. To the contrary, partially new 'inventions', because of this special feature they have, ie that they are not entirely new, should be considered on a case-by-case basis. This argument is supported by the fact that the industries that claim patentability for partially new inventions are crucial not only for the preservation of competition, but also –and most importantly- for the welfare of consumers and society at large. A free ticket to patentability should not be given. In that sense, and taking into consideration all of the implications of patentability in the sectors-in-question, a better balance should be sought between raising the stakes too high for the inventive step, on the one hand (as proven after Genentech), and having the stakes too low for patentability in general (in the sense that something partially new could be granted patentability as long as the inventive step requirement is fulfilled) when it comes to products/processes that are partially new.

United States v Camou: Warrantless Cell Phone Searches after *Riley v California*

Marco Y. Wong[1]

This Comment examines how the Fourth Amendment applies to warrantless cell phone searches in United States v Camou, *and questions whether the Ninth Circuit's ultimate position is desirable. Last year, in Riley v California, the United States Supreme Court held that a police officer should generally get a warrant before searching a defendant's cell phone incident to her arrest. It explained that cell phone searches may be very intrusive of one's privacy because of the amount of information that cell phones can contain, as well as their pervasiveness in our lives. The* Camou *court was challenged with what this insight meant for other exceptions to the Fourth Amendment's traditional warrant requirement. After discussing, in Part I,* Camou's *holding that evidence was improperly obtained and had to be excluded, Part II examines* Camou's *analyses of the exigency and automobile exceptions to the traditional warrant requirement, and good faith exception to the Fourth Amendment exclusionary rule. It suggests, in Part III, that the Supreme Court should reject exigency searches of cell phones altogether, endorse but further elaborate* Camou's *holding that cell phones are non-containers under the automobile exception, and reject its understanding of good faith. We should expand defendants' rights by requiring police to get a warrant in all cell phone searches—since it is quick and easy to do so—but constrain their remedy to include evidence where an officer relies on her own objectively reasonable mistakes or binding court*

---

[1] JD Candidate, Columbia Law School; LLB Candidate, London School of Economics and Political Science. I am grateful to Judge Debra A. Livingston for inspiring my interest in this area of the law, and to Judge Livingston, Professor I. Bennett Capers, and Professor Daniel C. Richman for invaluable feedback and conversations. I am also thankful to Michelle Bai, Christine Banta, Daniel Huang, Jerald Khoo, and Philippe Kuhn for their comments and assistance.

precedent—since the exclusionary rule's goal is to deter police misconduct.

Keywords: Cell phones, Fourth Amendment, *Riley v California*, exigency, automobiles, good faith, technology.

1. Introduction

The Fourth Amendment of the United States Constitution offers us protection against unreasonable searches and seizures of our persons, houses, papers, and effects.[2] While the Supreme Court has stated a preference for searches pursuant to lawfully obtained search warrants,[3] it has recognized a number of "exceptions" in which a warrantless search will be reasonable.[4] None of this is particularly new. What has challenged the courts over time, however, is the question of how this framework applies to continually changing technology.[5] Cell phones are particularly concerning—not only can a search of one's cell phone be more intrusive of privacy than a search of one's home, but the use of cell phones, unlike other forms of technology, has also become increasingly prevalent amongst the general populace.[6] In the face of this double whammy,

---

[2] US Const amend IV.

[3] *Thompson v Louisiana* 469 US 17, 20 (1984) ("[W]e have consistently reaffirmed our understanding that in all cases outside the exceptions to the warrant requirement the Fourth Amendment requires the interposition of a neutral and detached magistrate between the police and the 'persons, houses, papers, and effects' of citizens."). A search warrant is a document issued by a judicial officer, upon finding that the police have probable cause—defined as "fair probability"—to search a specified premises, and authorizing the police to do so. *Illinois v Gates* 462 US 213, 246 (1983).

[4] Referring to a warrantless search as an "exception" is a misnomer because the courts have recognized so many of them. Akhil R Amar, 'Fourth Amendment First Principles' (1994) 107 Harv L Rev 757, 762–771 ("We have now seen at least eight historical and commonsensical exceptions to the so-called warrant requirement. There are many others—but I am a lover of mercy."). See n 9, 35, 38.

[5] *United States v Jones* 132 S Ct 945 (2012) (concluding that installation of electronic tracking device to the defendant's wife's car was a Fourth Amendment search); *United States v Karo* 468 US 705 (1984) (finding that monitoring of a beeper in a private residence implicated the Fourth Amendment); *United States v White* 401 US 745 (1971) (holding that the law did not protect persons whose conversations with others are recorded and transmitted to the police).

[6] *Riley v California* 134 S Ct 2473, 2490 (2014) ("[N]early three-quarters of smart phone users report being within five feet of their phones most of the time, with 12% admitting that they even use their phones in the shower...many of the more than 90% of American adults who own a cell phone keep on their person a digital record of nearly every aspect of their lives—from the mundane to the intimate...[t]he average smart phone user has installed 33

how do we limit the state's ability to access our personal data? This Comment argues that requiring the police to get a warrant in all cell phone searches is the best way to restrain governmental access into our private lives. But given the harshness of the Fourth Amendment exclusionary rule,[7] evidence should not be excluded where an officer relies on her own objectively reasonable mistakes or *binding* court precedent.

In *Riley v California*,[8] the Supreme Court considered the question of whether search incident to arrest[9] ("SIA") applied to cell phones. There, the defendant was arrested for driving with expired registration tags.[10] Police officers obtained his cell phone from his pants, searched it, and found a number of text messages and videos implicating him in an unrelated shooting.[11] The court unanimously held that a warrant was generally required for cell phone searches.[12] The court observed that SIA's traditional justifications—ensuring officer safety and preventing evidence destruction—did not apply in the cell phone context. Phone data did not endanger officers as a weapon might have,[13] and the police could have easily prevented data loss by disconnecting the phone from the network.[14] Importantly, although the police could search car containers incident to arrest where it was reasonable to believe that evidence relevant to the crime of arrest might be found in the car,[15] cell phones were not containers. This is because cell phones could "access data located elsewhere, at the tap of a screen," and contain evidence

---

apps, which together can form a revealing montage of the user's life."); Orin S Kerr, 'Searches and Seizures in a Digital World' (2011) 119 Harv L Rev 531, 541–543 (2011) (observing that computers differ from houses in that they contain a staggering amount of data, most users do not know about and cannot control the storage of this information, and computer operating systems and programs generate and store a wealth of information about how the computer and its contents have been used).

[7] *Mapp v Ohio* 367 US 643 (1961) (holding that evidence obtained by searches and seizures in violation of the Constitution is inadmissible in state courts).

[8] *Riley v California* 134 S Ct 2473, 2473 (2014).

[9] "Search incident to arrest" is an "exception" to the warrant requirement that allows the police to search an arrestee's person, *United States v Robinson* 414 US 218 (1973). The police may search the arrestee's reachable space if the arrestee is in her home, *Chimel v California* 395 US 752 (1969). The police may also search the arrestee's car when the arrestee is unsecured and within reaching distance of the passenger compartment at the time of the search, and when it is reasonable to believe that evidence relevant to the crime of arrest might be found in the car, *Arizona v Gant* 129 S Ct 1710 (2009).

[10] *Riley v California* 134 S Ct 2473, 2480 (2014).

[11] *Ibid.*

[12] *Ibid.*, 2494.

[13] *Ibid.*, 2485–2486.

[14] *Ibid.*, 2486–2488 (discussing that the police can prevent remote wiping by (1) turning off the phone or removing its battery, or (2) leaving the phone powered on and placing it in an enclosure called a Faraday bag to isolate the phone from radio waves).

[15] See n 9.

of past crimes.[16] But while *Riley* decided the SIA issue, it deliberately left open the question of whether other "exceptions" to the warrant requirement could justify a warrantless search of one's cell phone.[17]

Since the Supreme Court's ruling, lower courts have grappled with the question of *Riley*'s scope, finding that some warrantless cell phone searches can still be constitutional.[18] This Comment investigates the Ninth Circuit's contribution to this discussion in *United States v Camou.*[19] After detailing the court's holding in Part 1, Part 2 examines *Camou*'s analyses of the exigency and automobile exceptions to the Fourth Amendment's traditional warrant requirement and good faith doctrine. It suggests, in Part III, that the Supreme Court should reject exigency searches of cell phones, endorse but further elaborate *Camou*'s holding that cell phones are non-containers under the automobile exception, and reject its understanding of good faith.

2. United States v Camou

In *Camou*, United States Border Patrol agents found an undocumented immigrant in the backseat of Camou's truck at a primary inspection checkpoint in Westmorland, California.[20] They arrested Camou, his girlfriend, and the immigrant, and seized Camou's truck and cell phone.[21] During the booking process, Agent Baldwin inventoried Camou's cell phone as "seized property and evidence."[22] One hour and twenty minutes after the arrest, Agent Walla searched Camou's cell phone for evidence of "known smuggling organizations and information related to the case."[23] He searched the call logs of the cell phone and found a number of calls from "Mother Teresa."[24] He

---

[16] *Riley v California* 134 S Ct 2473, 2491 (2014).

[17] *Ibid.,* 2494 (observing that "other case-specific exceptions may still justify a warrantless search of a particular phone," and referring to the exigency exception in particular).

[18] *United States v Dahl* Criminal Action No. 14-382, 2014 WL 6792676 (E.D. Pa. Dec. 3, 2014) (*Riley* does not overrule precedent allowing warrantless search of a probationer's cell phone based on reasonable suspicion); *United States v Saboonchi* 48 F Supp 3d 815 (D. Md. 2014) (*Riley* does not alter the reasonable suspicion standard for the border search of a smartphone and flashdrive).

[19] *United States v Camou* 773 F 3d 932 (9th Cir. 2014).

[20] *Ibid.,* 935.

[21] *Ibid.*

[22] *Ibid.*

[23] *Ibid.,* 936. There was arguably probable cause to search Camou's cell phone because his girlfriend informed Border Patrol that before picking up the undocumented immigrant, Camou received a phone call from someone who went by the alias "Mother Teresa," and during Camou's girlfriend's interview, Camou's cell phone rang several times, displaying a phone number on the screen which was identified as belonging to "Mother Teresa." *ibid.*

[24] *Ibid.*

then exited the call logs screen and searched the videos and photographs contained on the phone's internal memory.[25] He stopped reviewing the phone's contents after finding thirty to forty images of child pornography.[26]

Camou was tried for possession of child pornography.[27] The District Court for the Southern District of California denied his motion to suppress the child pornography images that Agent Walla found on his cell phone.[28] Judge Huff held that the search of the phone was a lawful SIA.[29] Alternatively, if the search were unconstitutional, she would have found that both good faith[30] and inevitable discovery[31] exceptions applied to prevent exclusion of the evidence.[32]

The Court of Appeals for the Ninth Circuit reversed the lower court's decision.[33] The court found that the passage of one hour and twenty minutes and a string of intervening acts between Camou's arrest and the cell phone search meant that the phone was not roughly contemporaneous with arrest to constitute an SIA.[34] The exigency[35] exception did not apply, because the agents were not faced with a "now or never situation" such as an imminent loss of evidence.[36] Even if exigencies existed, the scope of the search was impermissibly overbroad because it extended beyond call logs to include photographs and videos.[37] The automobile[38] exception did not apply.

---

[25] *Ibid.*

[26] *Ibid.*

[27] 18 USC §2252(a)(4)(B) (2012).

[28] *United States v Camou* 773 F 3d 932, 936 (9th Cir. 2014).

[29] *Ibid.*

[30] The "good faith exception" is an exception to the general rule that evidence is excluded if the police obtained it in violation of the Fourth Amendment. It applies where the police objectively relied on the error in good faith. *United States v Leon* 468 US 897 (1984). The good faith exception applied when the error leading to the Fourth Amendment violation was attributable to a non-police actor—for instance, a magistrate, *ibid.*; the legislature, *Illinois v Krull* 480 US 340 (1987); or a court clerk, *Arizona v Evans* 514 US 1 (1995).

[31] Like the "good faith exception", the "inevitable discovery exception" is an exception to the general rule that evidence is excluded if the police obtained it in violation of the Fourth Amendment. It applies where evidence would have been found anyway even if there were no Fourth Amendment violation. *Nix v Williams* 467 US 431 (1984).

[32] *Ibid.*

[33] *Ibid.*, 937.

[34] *Ibid.*, 939.

[35] Like SIA, "exigency" is an "exception" to the warrant requirement that allows the police to conduct a search without getting a warrant where there was not enough time to do so, as in cases involving fleeing suspects, *Warden v Hayden* 387 US 294 (2009); potential evidence loss, *United States v Elkins* 300 F 3d 638 (6th Cir. 2002); or threat of serious injury, *Brigham City v Stuart* 547 US 398 (2006).

[36] *Ibid.*, 941.

[37] *Ibid.*

Expressing concern with the intrusiveness of a cell phone search and that automobile exception searches were not limited by time or relevance, the court found that cell phones were non-containers.[39] Finally, the court held that neither inevitable discovery nor good faith exceptions applied. The former failed because the government did not show that it would have applied for a warrant to search Camou's phone for evidence of alien smuggling activity, and precedent prevented officers who had probable cause but simply did not try to get a search warrant from being excused from getting a warrant.[40] Nor did the good faith exception apply because the government did not demonstrate that Agent Walla relied on an external source.[41]

3. EXIGENCY, AUTOMOBILE EXCEPTION, GOOD FAITH

At first glance, *Camou* appears to be a simple and faithful application of precedent. However, on closer examination, the Ninth Circuit broke new ground in a number of ways. This section examines the court's pioneering efforts in its analyses of (A) the exigency exception, (B) the automobile exception, and (C) good faith. The court should have elaborated its holdings in each of these areas, because existing Supreme Court jurisprudence did not require its conclusions.

3.1. Exigency

Because *Camou* did not involve a situation where there was no time to get a warrant, the court was justified in concluding that there was no exigency.[42] If the agents were concerned about remote wiping of data on the cell phone, they should have turned off the cell phone, taken out its battery, and placed it in a Faraday bag.[43] If there was probable cause that evidence related to Camou's alien smuggling activity was on the cell phone, the agents should have submitted this information for a judicially authorized warrant.

The *Camou* court did not stop there, however. It added that even if there was an exigency, "the search's scope was impermissibly overbroad" because it went beyond contacts and call logs to include photographs and videos that

---

[38] Like SIA and exigency, the "automobile exception" is an "exception" to the warrant requirement. The police may conduct a warrantless search of a car where there is probable cause to believe that evidence is contained in it. *California v Acevedo* 500 US 565 (1991).

[39] *Ibid.*, 943.

[40] *United States v Camou* 773 F 3d 932, 944 (9th Cir. 2014).

[41] *Ibid.*, 945.

[42] See n 36.

[43] Text to n 14.

were stored on the phone's internal memory.[44] In the physical context, the principle that an exigency search must be strictly circumscribed by the exigencies which justify its initiation has long been accepted.[45] Consider the example of a warrantless entry into a home while a homicide is taking place ("the bedroom gunshot example"). If a gunshot is heard resounding from the upstairs bedroom, exigency allows the police to search the bedroom without a warrant. It does not, however, allow them also to search the basement unless they have a warrant or another exception to the warrant "requirement" applies.[46] The reason is twofold. First, the police may not have probable cause[47] to search the basement. Second, the police have time to get a search warrant.[48] Neither of these reasons—and it is not clear upon which of these the *Camou* court relies—justified the court's finding that the search's scope was impermissibly overbroad.

One possible reading of the court's statement is that Agent Walla only had probable cause to search the contacts and call logs. The court did not, however, explain why probable cause is limited this way in the search of Camou's cell phone. It is helpful to analogize to a physical search. Take the example of a warrantless search of a defendant who had a glassine bag containing narcotics and a memo book on his person ("the drugs and memo book example").[49] In that situation, the court would likely find that the police had probable cause not only as to the bag of drugs but also the memo book. This is because it is probable that the memo book would contain information about the defendant's contacts and transactions. Applying this understanding to *Camou*, the court appeared to draw a bright line between a phone's contacts and call logs, on the one hand, and its photographs and videos, on the other. But it is not immediately clear why "evidence of 'known smuggling organizations and information related to the case'" would not likely be found

---

[44] *United States v Camou* 773 F 3d 932, 941 (9th Cir. 2014).

[45] *Mincey v Arizona* 437 US 385 (1978).

[46] Text to n 4. In practice, courts have been more lenient in their interpretation of exigency, allowing officers to conduct a protective sweep where they "reasonably believed that a shooting victim or an additional armed suspect might be in the house." *United States v Goodrich* 739 F 3d 1091, 1096 (8th Cir. 2014).

[47] See n 4.

[48] A search warrant is favored because it offers a number of police power-constraining safeguards. To obtain a warrant, the police must demonstrate probable cause, under oath and affirmation, to a magistrate. The particularity requirement limits the legitimate scope of searches spatially and temporally. Once a warrant is obtained, there is a further safeguard that a warrant must be executed in a constitutionally acceptable way. *Wilson v Layne* 526 US 603 (1999) (holding that third parties are allowed during a search only if they are in aid of the execution of the warrant); *Wilson v Arkansas* 514 US 927 (1995) (recognizing that absent special justification, the police must knock and announce their identity).

[49] I am grateful to Judge Livingston for this example.

in one's photographs and videos.[50] One could reasonably believe that photographs of other smugglers and illegal immigrants,[51] or videos of the locations where smugglers met, would be found.[52] This information may be just as or more probative than a list of phone digits, especially since contacts' names on a cell phone may be concealed and, if prepaid cell phones were used,[53] contacts could be difficult to track.[54]

Another reading of the court's analysis is that Agent Walla should not have ventured beyond the contacts and call logs, regardless of whether there was probable cause to do so, because he had time to get a search warrant. While limiting a warrantless search in this way in a physical search may be sensible, a number of difficulties emerge in the context of an electronic search. How are officers to know when an exigency ends in the electronic search context? In the bedroom gunshot example, the exigency arguably ends when the occupants are subdued or handcuffed.[55] Similarly, in the drugs and memo book example, the exigency likely ends when the drugs and memo book have been removed from the defendant so that he is not able to destroy

---

[50] *United States v Camou* 773 F 3d 932, 936 (9th Cir. 2014).

[51] For examples of how photographs have been used to incriminate defendants, Nina Golgowski, 'London Drug Dealers Sentenced after Being Caught with Boastful Cellphone Photos of Drugs, Cash' *New York Daily News* (New York, 29 Oct. 2014) <http://www.nydailynews.com/news/world/london-drug-dealers-trophy-photos-drugs-cash-phones-article-1.1992100> accessed 13 May 2015; Mark Duell, 'Busted! Drug Smuggler Caught After He Spelled His Nickname in Cocaine while Posing for Mobile Phone Photograph' *Daily Mail* (London, 26 May 2013) <http://www.dailymail.co.uk/news/article-2331155/Drug-smuggler-spelt-nickname-cocaine-10-man-British-gang-jailed-total-92-years.html> accessed 13 May 2015.

[52] Smugglers have also used text messages to signal the presence of Border Patrol to others. Marc Lacey, 'Smugglers Guide Illegal Immigrants with Cues via Cellphone' *New York Times* (New York, 9 May 2011) <http://www.nytimes.com/2011/05/09/us/09coyotes.html?_r=0> accessed 13 May 2015.

[53] Jim Dwyer, 'It's Not Just Drug Dealers Who Buy Prepaid Phones' *New York Times* (New York, 28 May 2010) <http://www.nytimes.com/2010/05/30/nyregion/30about.html> accessed 13 May 2015.

[54] Associated Press, 'Lawmakers Seek to Crack Down on Prepaid Cell Phones that Abet Criminal and Terror Suspects' *Fox News* (New York, 8 June 2010) <http://www.foxnews.com/us/2010/06/08/lawmakers-crack-prepaid-cell-phones-abet-criminal-terror-suspects/> accessed 13 May 2015. cf Justin Peters, *Can Disposable "Burner" Cellphones Protect You From Government Surveillance?*, Slate (New York, 7 June 2013) <http://www.slate.com/blogs/crime/2013/06/07/verizon_nsa_scandal_can_disposable_burner_cell_phones_protect_you_from_government.html> accessed 13 May 2015 (observing that while prepaid phones "make it more difficult for the government to determine who you are," two qualifications render the phones "by no means untraceable": (1) calls made on prepaid phones are generally transmitted over existing networks, and (2) it is not hard for the government to determine one's location based on her phone's communication with cell towers).

[55] *Mincey v Arizona* 437 US 385 (1978).

the evidence.[56] A reasonable police officer would recognize that the exigencies presented in these cases have come to an end. The *Riley* response to when a cell phone exigency search terminates does not answer this question,[57] because the *Camou* court's discussion of impermissible overbreadth was premised on "the exigencies of the situation permit[ting] a search of Camou's cell phone to prevent the loss of call data."[58] In other words, *Camou* assumed for the purposes of its discussion that Agent Walla *could* look through the cell phone for exigency reasons. The court did not explain, however, why he was entitled to go as far as the contacts and call logs, but was constitutionally required to stop before perusing the photographs and videos. Absent any distinctive event terminating the exigency, as there was in both the bedroom gunshot and the drugs and memo book examples, an ordinary police officer without specialized technological training is unlikely to know what he is and is not entitled to do.[59] If, for instance, an officer were allowed to search a cell phone to prevent evidence destruction, at what point would this threat end and how would an ordinarily trained officer know? The *Riley* court may have had these challenges in mind when concluding that an officer should generally get a warrant before searching a cell phone.[60]

A third reading of the court's analysis is that Agent Walla could have searched some photographs and videos, but not so many of them. But if this is what the court meant, and *Camou* held that scrolling through *hundreds* of photographs and videos failed the "impermissibly overbroad" standard,[61] it is not clear what this means in a less extreme case involving a search of fewer photographs and videos. Nor did *State v Carroll*,[62] the only authority on which the court relied to reach its conclusion, mention how many images the police viewed on the defendant's cell phone.[63] The *Camou* court committed only one paragraph of its opinion to the impermissible overbreadth question, providing scant guidance for courts and law enforcement officers in the future.

---

[56] *United States v Elkins* 300 F 3d 638 (6th Cir. 2002).

[57] Text to n 14.

[58] *United States v Camou* 773 F 3d 932, 941 (9th Cir. 2014).

[59] Kerr, 'Searches and Seizures in a Digital World' (n 6) 574–576 (concluding that ex post standards are favored over ex ante rules because "the computer forensics process is contingent, fact-bound, and quite unpredictable," so that "even a skilled forensic expert cannot predict exactly what techniques will be necessary to find the information sought by a warrant".).

[60] *Riley v California* 134 S Ct 2473, 2485 (2014).

[61] *United States v Camou* 773 F 3d 932, 941 (9th Cir. 2014).

[62] *State v Carroll* 778 N W 2d 1, 12 (Wis. 2010).

[63] Because there was no reference to the quantity of images perused by the police in Carroll's holding at all, this interpretation of *Camou*'s holding is least probable.

3.2. Automobile Exception

The traditional justification for the automobile exception is that because cars are highly moveable, evidence would be lost by the time that police officers are able to secure a warrant.[64] Over time, this rationale has changed—the warrantless search of a car is now justified because one has a reduced expectation of privacy in one's car.[65] So long as there is probable cause to search a car, the police are entitled to search containers and passengers' belongings that are capable of concealing the object of a search,[66] even though this can lead to anomalous results.[67] The question that *Camou* faced was whether a cell phone was considered a container.[68]

The *Camou* court concluded that there was "no reason not to extend the reasoning in *Riley*," holding that cell phones were not containers in the SIA context, to the automobile exception.[69] If we take the question of "what is a container" in isolation, the court's logic is attractive. In both SIA and automobile exception contexts, analyzing a cell phone as a container is strained as a matter of language.[70] Also under both circumstances, searching a cell phone implicates significant privacy concerns because of the amount of information that cell phones contain.[71] Finally, the definition of "container" is the same for *physical* evidence in both SIA and automobile exception cases.[72] As a matter of literal language, the court seemed justified to find that cell phones were non-containers.

Two differences should be observed, however. First, whereas the government did not have probable cause in relation to the cell phone in *Riley*, it did in *Camou*. In *Riley*, the police had probable cause to arrest the defendant, but no probable cause to search either his person or cell phone. Police officers were entitled to search the defendant's person in that case not because they had probable cause, but because of the *Robinson* bright-line rule

---

[64] *Carroll v United States* 267 US 132 (1925).

[65] *California v Carney* 471 US 386 (1985).

[66] *Wyoming v Houghton* 526 US 295 (1999); *California v Acevedo* 500 US 565, 579 (1991) ("We conclude that it is better to adopt one clear-cut rule to govern automobile searches and eliminate the warrant requirement for closed containers".).

[67] *California v Acevedo* 500 US 565, 581 (1991) ("[I]t is anomalous to prohibit a search of a briefcase while the owner is carrying it exposed on a public street yet to permit a search once the owner has placed the briefcase in the locked trunk of his car".).

[68] *United States v Camou* 773 F 3d 932, 942 (9th Cir. 2014).

[69] *Ibid.*

[70] *Riley v California* 134 S Ct 2473, 2491 (2014).

[71] Text to n 6.

[72] *New York v Belton* 453 US 454, 460 (1981) ("'Container' here denotes any object capable of holding another object. It thus includes closed or open glove compartments, consoles, or other receptacles located anywhere within the passenger compartment, as well as luggage, boxes, bags, clothing, and the like".).

that the police could search an arrestee's person.[73] In *Camou*, by contrast, the agents had probable cause to search the car and any containers and passengers' belongings that could contain evidence of smuggling.[74] Since a cell phone may plausibly contain evidence of smuggling such as contacts and other information,[75] Agent Walla had probable cause to search it if it were a container.

Second, the court did not give enough attention to the different rationales that underlay the two doctrines. The court correctly observed that the justifications for these two warrant requirement exceptions were different. SIA was "rooted in arrest and the *Chimel* rationales of preventing arrestees from harming officers and destroying evidence [while] the vehicle exception [was] instead motivated by the supposedly lower expectation of privacy individuals [had] in their vehicles as well as the mobility of vehicles."[76] The court also correctly found that this difference meant that the one hour and twenty minute delay, while fatal to the state's SIA argument, did not defeat the automobile exception argument.[77] But the court did not take this difference into account when deciding whether to extend *Riley*'s holding that cell phones were non-containers under SIA to searches under the automobile exception.

In *Riley*, the court weighed the twin SIA justifications with the consequences of allowing a warrantless cell phone search. Since there were no officer safety or evidence preservation interests involved (minimal benefits) and significant privacy interests were implicated (high costs), the court concluded that cell phones fell outside SIA's coverage.[78] The *Camou* court should have engaged in a balancing analysis rather than accept *Riley*'s outcome because the factors in play in *Camou* were different. While significant privacy interests were still involved (high costs), the other side of the scale included that Camou had a lessened privacy expectation in his car, and that the state had an interest in getting probative evidence to build its case (high benefits).[79] It is plausible that the court might have reached the opposite conclusion after engaging in this balancing exercise. The court, however, swept these distinctions aside without elaborating on its policy choice.

---

[73] See n 4.
[74] *United States v Camou* 773 F 3d 932, 942 (9th Cir. 2014) ("We assume that the agents had probable cause to believe Camou's truck contained evidence of criminal activity once they saw Martinez-Ramirez lying down behind the seats of the truck".).
[75] Text to n 51–52.
[76] *Ibid.*, 941.
[77] *Ibid.*, 942.
[78] *Riley v California* 134 S Ct 2473, 2493–2495 (2014).
[79] *United States v Camou* 773 F 3d 932, 941–943 (9th Cir. 2014).

3.3. Good Faith

In *Herring v United States*,[80] the Supreme Court held that the good faith exception applied where the violation was attributable to a police employee, so long as it was not "deliberate," "reckless," "grossly negligent," or "recurring or systemic negligence."[81] The *Camou* court, however, interpreted *Herring* to draw a line between the officer's own acts and a third party's acts. According to the Ninth Circuit, the good faith exception only applied in the latter scenario.[82] Since Agent Walla did not rely on someone else's error, the good faith exception was inapplicable in *Camou.*[83]

As a matter of precedent, it is unlikely that the Supreme Court intended to draw the line between officers' reliance on their own actions and their reliance on third party actions. This is because courts have repeatedly held that the rationale underlying the exclusionary rule is to deter police misconduct.[84] Excluding the evidence in a case where an officer relies on his mistaken and reasonable belief does not further this goal. First, to pass the *Herring* standard, the officer's conduct had to be something less than recurring or systemic negligence.[85] This means that the officer who *purposely* made a mistake, the officer who *knew of a risk* that he was making a mistake, and the officer who *did not know (but should have known) of a risk* that he was making a mistake *and made "routine or widespread" mistakes* would be treated the same way. In all three cases, the evidence would be excluded. *Camou* held an officer by an even more rigorous standard—if she made and relied on her own mistake, the evidence was excluded, even if the mistake was reasonably made.[86] Yet it

---

[80] *Herring v United States* 555 US 135 (2009).
[81] *ibid.*, 144.
[82] *United States v Camou* 773 F 3d 932, 945 (9th Cir. 2014).
[83] *ibid.*
[84] *United States v Spears* 31 F Supp 3d 869, 874 (N.D. Tex. 2014) ("The sole purpose of the exclusionary rule is to deter culpable law enforcement conduct."); *People v Rodriguez* A134782 & A138665, 2014 WL 5509829, at *8 (Cal. App. 1st. Nov. 3, 2014) ("The purpose of the rule is to deter further Fourth Amendment violations".); *People v Allen* No. B245581, 2014 WL 5469894, at *6 (Cal. App. 2nd. Oct. 29, 2014) ("To deter such conduct by law enforcement, the U.S. Supreme Court created the exclusionary rule."). cf *Herring v United States* 555 US 135, 152 (2009) ("[T]he rule also serves other important purposes: It enables the judiciary to avoid the taint of partnership in official lawlessness, and it assures the people—all potential victims of unlawful government conduct—that the government would not profit from its lawless behavior, thus minimizing the risk of seriously undermining popular trust in government".) (Ginsburg, J., dissenting); *United States v Stephens* 764 F 3d 327 (4th Cir. 2014) ("The Government must err on the side of the Constitution and obtain a warrant especially as the disturbing specter of Government agents hiding electronic devices in all sorts of personal property and then following private citizens who own such property as they go about their business becomes ever more possible".) (Thacker, J., dissenting).
[85] *Herring v United States* 555 US 135, 147 (2009).
[86] *United States v Camou* 773 F 3d 932, 945 (9th Cir. 2014).

is unlikely that an officer who made a reasonable mistake could be deterred from making another mistake in the future.[87] Second, in addition to failing to deter police misconduct, *Camou* may over-deter proper police action. Officers may be disincentivized from acting on their own understandings where there exists the slightest hint of doubt, in fear that evidence collected will be excluded.[88] Third, *Camou* may ultimately have negligible effect on defendants whose Fourth Amendment rights are violated if officers respond to it by increasing their reliance on their colleagues' understandings. This loophole allows officers to act upon negligent beliefs, so long as they can point to someone else as the originator of those beliefs. The own act/third party act line generates particularly anomalous results where an officer's own beliefs turn out to be more objectively reasonable than a third party's beliefs, as for instance where a more experienced officer seeks advice from a less experienced officer.

Even if the officer could rely on his own isolated and attenuated acts, the *Camou* court observed that the "governing law at the time of the search made clear that a search incident to arrest had to be contemporaneous with the arrest."[89] If the law were clear at the time of the search and Agent Walla acted contrary to it, then the court would be justified in finding that the good faith exception did not apply. In *Davis v United States*,[90] the Supreme Court considered an officer's reliance on binding appellate precedent. There, an officer conducted an SIA of a car under the authority of *New York v Belton*.[91] *Belton* established a bright line rule that permitted police officers to search the passenger compartment of a car including containers following a lawful custodial arrest of a car occupant.[92] The *Belton* rule was later overturned by the Supreme Court in *Arizona v Gant*.[93] The *Davis* court held that the good

---

[87] *Herring v United States* 555 US 135, 144–147 (2009) ("To trigger the exclusionary rule, police conduct must be sufficiently deliberate that exclusion can meaningfully deter it, and sufficiently culpable that such deterrence is worth the price paid by the justice system.").

[88] Note, 'Toward a General Good Faith Exception' (2013) 127 Harv L Rev 773 ("If the extreme remedy of suppression were available only when police commit a clear violation of the Constitution—when it is unreasonable to think the search reasonable—officers would become less likely to abandon perfectly lawful searches out of an abundance of caution."). Laura E Collins, '*Davis v United States*: Expanding the Good Faith Exception to the Exclusionary Rule to Objective Reliance on Binding Appellate Precedent Presents Too Many Threats to Constitutional Protections' (2012) 81 Miss LJ 163, 192 ("If police officers know wrongfully obtained evidence will be thrown out, they may become too cautious in investigations, leaving valuable evidence unfound.").

[89] *ibid.*, 944–945.

[90] *Davis v United States* 131 S Ct 2419 (2011).

[91] *New York v Belton* 453 US 454 (1981).

[92] *Ibid.*, 459–460.

[93] See n 4.

faith exception to the exclusionary rule applied.[94] But while *Camou* cited precedent stating that an SIA had to be contemporaneous with the arrest,[95] it is not clear how the reasonable officer could have known that the automobile exception would not apply.[96] Moreover, the search occurred in 2009,[97] before *Riley* provided authoritative guidance on how the police should handle cell phones in an SIA.[98]

It may be that the Ninth Circuit was reading *Davis* as holding that the good faith exception only applied where binding precedent existed. If this were the case, it was immaterial that there was no case law on whether an officer could search a cell phone pursuant to the automobile or SIA exceptions. That there was no precedent to which an officer could point would mean that she must err on the side of caution and not conduct the search. If this was how the court interpreted *Davis*, it should have been more explicit because other courts' interpretations of *Davis* have varied significantly.[99] While some have read *Davis* as limited to reliance on binding appellate

---

[94] *Davis v United States* 131 S Ct 2419, 2423–2424 (2011).

[95] *United States v Camou* 773 F.3d 932, 944–945 (9th Cir. 2014).

[96] Orin S Kerr, 'Cell Phone Exempt from the Automobile Search Exception, Ninth Circuit Rules' (The Volokh Conspiracy, 11 Dec. 2014) <http://www.washingtonpost.com/news/volokh-conspiracy/wp/2014/12/11/cell-phones-exempt-from-the-automobile-search-*exception*-ninth-circuit-rules/> accessed 13 May 2015. There is, moreover, language in Supreme Court jurisprudence suggesting that officers could search any container in a car. *California v Acevedo* 500 US 565, 579–580 (1991) ("The scope of a warrantless search of an automobile…is not defined by the nature of the container in which the contraband is secreted. Rather, it is defined by the object of the search and the places in which there is probable cause to believe that it may be found".).

[97] *United States v Camou* 773 F.3d 932, 935–936 (9th Cir. 2014).

[98] See Introduction.

[99] cf *United States v McCane* 573 F 3d 1037, 1045 (10th Cir. 2009) ("Relying upon the settled case law of a United States Court of Appeals certainly qualifies as objectively reasonable law enforcement behavior."), and *United States v Clark* 29 F Supp 3d 1131, 1137 (E.D. Tenn. 2014) (despite the "relative ease of asking for either consent or a warrant in the absence of an emergency situation", the officer's reliance on Supreme Court authority for searches of other types of containers found on the arrestee's person, and decisions of circuit courts on cell phone SIA, was "objectively reasonable".); with *United States v Loera* No. CR 13-1876 JB, 2014 WL 5859072, at *79 (D.N.M. Oct. 20, 2014) ("[T]o exclude evidence simply because law enforcement fell short of relying on binding appellate precedent would violate the Supreme Court's mandate that suppression should occur in only unusual circumstances: when it furthers the purposes of the exclusionary rule".) and *United States v Lopez* 895 F Supp 2d 592, 605 (D. Del. 2012) (holding that the good faith exception applied because officers "acted in reasonable reliance on the absence of federal or state case law establishing that GPS monitoring of a vehicle in public is a Fourth Amendment 'search'".). Orin S Kerr, 'Lower Court Interpretations of *Davis v United States* 131 S Ct 2419 (2011)' (The Volokh Conspiracy, 14 Aug. 2013) <http://volokh.com/2013/08/14/lower-court-interpretations-of-davis-v-united-states-131-s-ct-2419-2011/> accessed 13 May 2015.

precedent,[100] others have read it as applicable even where precedent was not binding.[101] In effect, those latter courts actualized Justice Breyer's fears in *Davis* that the good faith exception threatened to "swallow the exclusionary rule."[102] The Ninth Circuit may be trying to protect defendants' Fourth Amendment rights from further erosion. Yet nowhere in the *Camou* court's analysis of the good faith exception did it cite *Davis*, examine and discuss the extensive post-*Davis* case law, or otherwise seek to justify its position.

To summarize, the Ninth Circuit in *Camou* contributed a number of novel ideas to Fourth Amendment discourse in a deceptively concise judgment. Its analyses of exigency, the automobile exception, and good faith doctrine included a handful of concepts that, before now, were not decided. This is the case despite the court's outcome appearing to be a necessary corollary of existing precedent.

4. Restoring Clarification to Cell Phone Searches

At the time of this Comment, eight cases have considered *Camou*'s scope. Four of them cited *Camou* to reinforce propositions of Fourth Amendment law that have been widely accepted and are not challenged in this paper. *United States v Salazar*[103] cited *Camou* as authority that the police may not search a cell phone incident to arrest absent exigency;[104] *Vito Bruno v Donat*,[105] that a search incident to lawful arrest is not violative of the Fourth Amendment;[106] *State v Meitler*,[107] that an exigency search must be based on

---

[100] *United States v Martin* 712 F 3d 1080, 1082 (7th Cir. 2013) ("We reject the government's invitation to allow police officers to rely on a diffuse notion of the weight of authority around the country, especially where that amorphous opinion turns out to be incorrect in the Supreme Court's eyes.").

[101] *United States v Katzin* 769 F 3d 163, 182 (3d Cir. 2014) (finding that the good faith exception applied because "[t]he constellation of circumstances that appeared to authorize [police] conduct included well settled principles of Fourth Amendment law as articulated by the Supreme Court, a near-unanimity of circuit courts applying these principles to the same conduct, and the advice of an AUSA pursuant to a DOJ-wide policy".).

[102] *Davis v United States* 131 S Ct 2419, 2439 (2011) ("But an officer who conducts a search that he believes complies with the Constitution but which, it ultimately turns out, falls just outside the Fourth Amendment's bounds is no more culpable than an officer who follows erroneous 'binding precedent.' Nor is an officer more culpable where circuit precedent is simply suggestive rather than 'binding,' where it only describes how to treat roughly analogous instances, or where it just does not exist". (Breyer, J., dissenting).

[103] *United States v Salazar* 598 Fed Appx 490 (9th Cir. 2015).

[104] *ibid.*, 491.

[105] *Vito Bruno v Donat* No. 3:09–cv–00165–RCJ–VPC, 2015 WL 1320925, at *15 (D. Nev. Mar. 24, 2015).

[106] *ibid.*, *15.

[107] *State v Meitler* 347 P 3d 670 (Kan. Ct. App. 2015).

probable cause;[108] and *United States v Washington*,[109] that the police may not rely on the inevitable discovery doctrine where they could have but chose not to obtain a search warrant.[110] These cases are at least mildly problematic because they do not recognize that *Camou* actually represents a significant change in the law.

More concerning are three of the post-*Camou* cases which support *Camou*'s good faith analysis. Judge Denny Chin's dissent in *United States v Raymonda*,[111] *Blair v United States*[112] in a footnote,[113] and most recently, *State v Thomas*,[114] have all endorsed the Ninth Circuit's novel own act/third party act distinction.[115] Since, as examined in Part II(C), the Ninth Circuit's holding in this area is unsupported by either precedent or policy, these cases' unquestioning acceptance of *Camou*'s good faith analysis is worrisome.

Even more alarming is *United States v Alonso-Castaneda*,[116] which applied *Camou*'s holdings—on exigency, automobiles, and good faith—in full force. There, a United States Border Patrol agent searched Alonso-Castaneda's cell phone during a car search for drugs-related evidence. First, in considering whether the exigency exception applied, but without clearly explaining what impermissible overbreadth meant, the District Court of Arizona found that the search was, like in *Camou*, impermissibly overbroad.[117] Next, in its discussion of the automobile exception, the court relied on *Camou*'s holding that cell phones were non-containers without asking whether *Camou*'s analysis was adequate.[118] Lastly, in rejecting the government's good faith argument, the court applied *Camou*'s own act/third party act distinction, without considering

---

[108] *ibid.*, *11.
[109] *United States v Washington* No. 2:14–CR–262 JCM (GWF), 2015 WL 1540486 (D. Nev. Apr. 2, 2015).
[110] *ibid.*, *15.
[111] *United States v Raymonda* 780 F 3d 105, 125 (2d Cir. 2015).
[112] *Blair v United States* No. 12–CF–1351, 2015 WL 2120329 (D.C. May 7, 2015).
[113] *ibid.*, *6 n.22. Even Professor LaFave's treatise, on which the *Blair* court relies, admits that his interpretations of what *Herring* means have their difficulties. Wayne R. LaFave, *Search and Seizure: A Treatise on the Fourth Amendment* (first published 1978, 5th edn, Thomson Reuters/West 2012) 299.
[114] *State v Thomas* No. 14AP–185, 2015 WL 2191107 (Ohio Ct. App. May 12, 2015).
[115] *ibid.*, *11–12.
[116] *United States v Alonso-Castaneda* No. CR–11–4067–TUC–DCB (BGM), 2015 WL 1711989 (D. Ariz. Apr. 15, 2015).
[117] *ibid.*, *7 ("Agent Kouris testified that he looked at the cellular telephone for text messages or calls relevant to the crime, or incriminating photographs of drugs, money, or weapons…This goes beyond any arguably permissible search to prevent the loss of call data".).
[118] *ibid.*, ("The Ninth Circuit Court of Appeals, however, has explicitly held 'that cell phones are not containers for purposes of the vehicle exception.' Accordingly, the search of Defendant Alonso-Castaneda's cell phone cannot be justified under the vehicle exception to the warrant requirement".).

whether the case was correctly decided.[119] Although it is still early, the post-*Camou* jurisprudence so far has shown no signs that lower courts will untie the knots of *Camou* on their own. In this light, Supreme Court intervention to restore coherence in this area of law is deeply welcome.

If an exigency search is permitted, the Supreme Court should elaborate what these limits are and justify them.[120] On balance, however, the court would probably be better off rejecting exigency searches of cell phones altogether. First, drawing lines in the electronic context inevitably leads to over and under-inclusiveness.[121] Second, cell phone searches pose an intrusive threat to our privacy.[122] Third, limits that apply in physical searches do not apply in the electronic context.[123] Finally, a warrant is not a heavy burden to impose in light of the "ease and speed with which search warrants nowadays can be obtained."[124] In short, the only reasonable search of a cell phone should be one pursuant to a warrant.

Since the question of whether cell phones are containers in the automobile exception context was undecided before *Camou*,[125] the Ninth Circuit was entitled to reach its conclusion that they were not. The court's choice may

---

[119] *ibid.*, *8 ("The Ninth Circuit Court of Appeals squarely addressed and rejected the Government's argument in this case. Agent Kouris did not rely 'on anyone or anything in conducting his search of [Defendant Alonso–Castaneda's] cell phone, let alone that any reliance was reasonable.' As such, the good faith exception is inapplicable to this case".).

[120] Samuel Beutler, 'The New World of Mobile Communication: Redefining the Scope of Warrantless Cell Phone Searches Incident to Arrest' (2013) 15 Vand J Ent & Tech L 375, 401 (proposing a function-based rule under which "a law enforcement officer would be allowed to search an arrestee's call log, text messages, and address book, but nothing more".).

[121] Patrick Brown, 'Searches of Cell Phones Incident to Arrest: Overview of the Law as it Stands and a New Path Forward' (2014) 27 Harv J L & Tech 563, 580 ("[I]t seems unclear under Beutler's proposed rule why…other cell phone contents with clear physical analogues like notes or photographs would not be [searchable]. Moreover, text message contents are a close analogue to the telephone conversations protected under Smith and should merit similar protections".). Albert Alschuler, 'Bright Line Fever and the Fourth Amendment' (1984) 45 U Pitt L Rev 227 (concluding that having too many categorical rules in Fourth Amendment law has led to incomprehensibility).

[122] Text to n 6.

[123] William J Stuntz, 'Race, Class, and Drugs' (1998) 97 Colum L Rev 1795, 1821 (arguing that police investigations are ordinarily constrained by limited resources and time); Adam Gershowitz, 'The iPhone Meets the Fourth Amendment' (2008) 56 UCLA L Rev 27 ("[N]ew technology inverts the typical state of affairs because it is the individual, not the police officer, who has the new technology…unlike flyovers or costly thermal imaging devices, the technology is everywhere".).

[124] *Fernandez v California* 134 S Ct 1126, 1142 (2014) (Ginsburg, J., dissenting).

[125] *United States v Burgess* 576 F 3d 1078, 1090 (10th Cir. 2009) (considering but ultimately not reaching a conclusion on the issue because "[i]nteresting as the issue may be, we need not now resolve it because the search of Burgess' hard drives was authorized by a warrant".).

have been the preferable one.[126] Were it otherwise, officers would easily be able to come up with reasons to search cell phones in the car and find vast amounts of evidence of other crimes, seriously intruding upon our privacy.[127] On the other hand, excluding cell phones from the automobile exception search leads to anomalous results where a physical document may be seized but the same document in electronic form is protected.[128] On balance, the court's conclusion was probably the better one, because of the sheer magnitude of private information that cell phones can hold.[129] The court should, however, be more honest in its reasoning, and dispel any impression that *Riley*'s holding automatically extends to *Camou*.

To restore nationwide uniformity, the Supreme Court should clarify what *Herring* and *Davis* stand for by explicitly endorsing or rejecting *Camou*'s position. In light that the good faith exception has long been rooted in deterrence of police misconduct,[130] it should overrule *Camou*'s interpretation of *Herring* as establishing a distinction between own and third party acts. The court should, however, limit *Davis* to *binding* precedent. Absent clear law authorizing the police to act, officers should err on the side of caution. This would allow the police some latitude when they make a mistake, without opening the Pandora's box that Justice Breyer viewed as the inevitable corollary of *Davis*.[131]

5. Conclusion

Riley and its progeny represent efforts by courts to retain the traditional Fourth Amendment architecture while adapting to rapid technological advances. After *Riley*, the Supreme Court left open a number of questions: (1) what limitations, if any, exist to constrain the scope of probable cause in exigency searches of a cell phone?; (2) should we extend *Riley*'s

---

[126] Marty Koresawa, 'Pay Phone Protections in a Smartphone Society: The Need to Restrict Searches of Modern Technology Incident to Arrest' (2012) 45 Loy LA L Rev 1351, 1387–1388 (concluding that cell phones should not be treated as containers).

[127] Elizabeth E Joh, 'Discretionless Policing: Technology and the Fourth Amendment' (2007) 95 Calif L Rev 199, 206 ("[D]iscretion in law enforcement is usually exercised covertly and with minimal oversight".). Illya Lichtenberg, 'Police Discretion and Traffic Enforcement' (2003) 50 Clev St L Rev 425 (observing that *Whren* gives the police, in effect, "unbridled discretion to stop any motorist" since "virtually every motorist is violating the law").

[128] *Riley v California* 134 S Ct 2473, 2497 (2014) (observing that "the Court's broad holding favors information in digital form over information in hard-copy form…[which] leads to anomalies," but joins the holding of the Court because he "do[es] not see a workable alternative") (Alito, J., concurring).

[129] Text to n 6.

[130] Text to n 84.

[131] Text to n 102.

intuition that "cell phones are different" to other exceptions to the warrant requirement?; and (3) if officers make a mistake regarding searches, what leeway, if any, should we allow them?

The *Camou* decision answered these questions by requiring that exigency searches not be impermissibly overbroad, finding that cell phones are not containers for automobile exception purposes, and suggesting that the good faith exception to the exclusionary rule should only apply where an officer relies on a negligent third party actor. Despite the matter-of-fact way in which the court dealt with these issues, it is not obvious from previous case law that these results necessarily follow. These complexities should not be ignored, but combated head on. To answer (1) and (2), this Comment has argued that the Supreme Court should, out of recognition that "cell phones are different," prohibit warrantless searches of cell phones altogether. As for (3), officers should be entitled to rely on their own objectively reasonable mistakes and binding precedent, both nothing beyond. As time progresses, we will constantly be challenged with the question of whether our existing legal frameworks can accommodate rapidly changing technological developments. For now, in the cell phone context, the answer is that they can. But one can imagine a world in which these premises no longer hold—if, for instance, criminals come up with ways to destroy evidence on a phone even when placed in a Faraday bag, or turn cell phones into weapons that can be launched from afar. In that world, we would need to critically rethink *Riley*, and it may be that our Constitution can no longer give us a satisfactory answer.

Legal Issues is operated by volunteers and relies on donations.
To support the Journal or UKLSA in general, email president@uklsa.co.uk.

If you are interested in joining the editorial board as an editor, reviewer, copy-editor, or formatting editor, email editor@uklsa.co.uk

Website: http://www.uklsa.co.uk
Facebook: https://www.facebook.com/UKLSA
Twitter: https://twitter.com/UKLSA

www.ingramcontent.com/pod-product-compliance
Lightning Source LLC
LaVergne TN
LVHW082347200926
848481LV00012B/3485